PRAISE FOR COLETTE BARON-REID
AND *Remembering the Future*

"In this utterly compelling book, you'll find yourself traveling with Colette Baron-Reid through her life as she evolves into one of the world's most remarkable psychics . . . and best of all—with simple yet powerful exercises—she shows you how to activate your own intuitive abilities as well. I highly recommend it!"

— **Denise Linn,** the best-selling author of
If I Can Forgive, So Can You

"I have personally consulted with Colette, and I find her to be 100 percent credible."
— **Dr. Wayne W. Dyer,**
The New York Times best-selling author of
Change Your Thoughts—Change Your Life

Remembering
the
future

Remembering the future

THE PATH TO RECOVERING INTUITION

COLETTE BARON-REID

HAY HOUSE, INC.
Carlsbad, California • New York City
London • Sydney • Johannesburg
Vancouver • Hong Kong • New Delhi

Published and distributed in the United States by: Hay House, Inc.:
www.hayhouse.com • *Published and distributed in Australia by:* Hay
House Australia Pty. Ltd.: www.hayhouse.com.au • *Published and distributed in the United Kingdom by:* Hay House UK, Ltd.: www.hayhouse.
co.uk • *Published and distributed in the Republic of South Africa by:*
Hay House SA (Pty), Ltd.: www.hayhouse.co.za • *Distributed in Canada
by:* Raincoast: www.raincoast.com • *Published in India by:* Hay House
Publishers India: www.hayhouse.co.in

Editorial supervision: Jill Kramer • *Design:* Tricia Breidenthal

Library of Congress Cataloging-in-Publication Data

Baron-Reid, Colette.
  Remembering the future : the path to recovering intuition / Colette
Baron-Reid.
      p. cm.
  Includes bibliographical references.
  ISBN-13: 978-1-4019-1041-9 (tradepaper)
  ISBN-10: 1-4019-1041-6 (tradepaper)
  1. Baron-Reid, Colette. 2. Intuition--Miscellanea. 3. Spiritual life--
Miscellanea. I. Title.
  BF1999.B3748167 2006
  133.8092--dc22
  [B]
                                    2006013282

ISBN 13: 978-1-4019-1041-9
ISBN 10: 1-4019-1041-6

11 10 09 08   7 6 5 4
1st printing, September 2006
4th printing, March 2008

Printed in the United States of America

For Mom, Dad, and Evelyn.
I miss you.

Author's Note: This book is a true recollection and account of my personal experiences and processes as they pertain to intuition and related spiritual phenomena. Some of the details have been altered for privacy, and names have only been included with written permission. In the tradition of anonymity, much of the story concerning my recovery from alcoholism/addiction is excluded, although it was—and continues to be—the spiritual bedrock upon which my life has flourished, one day at a time.

Contents

"And here is my secret. And it is a simple secret—it is only with the heart that one can see rightly. What is essential is invisible to the eye."

— Antoine de Saint-Exupéry

Introduction

For many years I've spent most of my waking hours searching for the meaning of the profound intuitive experiences that I've had since I was a child. These phenomena have all pointed to the undeniable fact that there's more to reality than what we're taught (or allowed) to perceive.

Since I was little, I've struggled to articulate something that seemed ordinary and natural to me yet wasn't so easily accepted by those around me. For a great part of my life, this lack of understanding on the part of others caused me to feel deeply confused and incredibly alone. While I felt isolated, I was struggling to make sense of something that I believed had to do with a profound connection to something vast and meaningful—and I know now that others shared my experience.

Looking back on the journey that took me from a difficult childhood filled with intrusive prescient dreams about my mother and grandfather, through my 17 years as a successful intuitive counselor, I see that life has afforded me some extraordinary epiphanies and experiences. I've found some answers to things that were secret and hidden, and I'm going to share what I've discovered with you in this book. I hope that it will make you think about, and realize, who you really are: a spirit in human form, with six senses—not just five—and all of the responsibility that this gift entails.

What's in a Name?

It's important to note that in this book I'm using the word *intuitive* rather than *psychic* when I refer to the sixth sense. I do this for a number of reasons. Over time, specific words tend to collect meanings and become burdened with stereotypes—*psychic* is one of them. Many people are fearful of this term, as it conjures up images of the supernatural such as crystal balls, witches, gypsy curses, cauldrons, and spells. And the fraudulent use of this gift by individuals who have not done their spiritual homework has made society even more suspicious.

Personally, I find the word *psychic* fascinating. It comes from the Greek *psychikos,* which means "of the soul." And although most would argue that having a soul is a very real part of being human, many of us are taught—in both obvious and subtle ways—to view the psychic and spiritual realms with suspicion and fear.

Most of us are taught that our physical bodies are houses of the soul. We also assume that our thoughts and consciousness are contained inside our heads. Suppose that isn't true? What if the soul was the house in which the body lives? What might this imply? I believe the soul only knows unity with the Divine. If this is so, why do we mostly see what appears to divide us?

I've never heard someone say that he or she was afraid of intuition or speak in hushed tones when discussing it. Most people are quite comfortable with the term, considering it an adjunct to their five senses. They acknowledge it as something uncanny and inexplicable that happens once in a while, rarely giving it additional thought. Most people own the word *intuitive* but disown *psychic,* assuming that they're different—one natural, the other supernatural—yet they're the same.

Some people are afraid of anything remotely psychic, as it presents an uncontrollable, intrusive mystery, something that holds power and is therefore dangerous. And sadly, because this force isn't understood (since it varies from person to person and doesn't obey the laws of intellect, hard science, reason, and logic), it remains tragically hidden away. If it's talked about at all, it's usually taboo or distorted through fear.

Still, if we assume that we're spiritual beings having a human experience that involves matters of the soul, then to be psychic is, in effect, to be human. As a result of basic ignorance, cultural bias, and religious superstition, the word *psychic*—although fundamentally referring to the soul—is generally thought of as a concept outside the realm of our daily experience. The consequences of this perceived separation are enormous for society and have ultimately led to the repression of all things psychic.

So, I stress that I've replaced the word *psychic* with *intuitive* strictly as a means to help people own their birthright to a sixth sense. However, these two terms are absolutely interchangeable.

My Experience, Strength, and Hope

In the first part of this book, I share my personal journey from struggle to denial to surrender, which finally led
me to recover my relationship with my own intuition.
In the second part, I show you how intuition is experienced, the way it works, where six-sensory information
comes from, and what it implies on a larger spiritual scale.
I explain the mechanics of it, and then I lead you through
a practical, spiritually principled program to "clean house"
before engaging you in exercises that will strengthen and
heighten your intuitive awareness.

I know that this process works, and once you begin, I
expect that you'll be amazed by your own intuitive awakening. The path to recovering intuition is the way to regaining
your wholeness and a true sense of spirituality: It gives you
the ability and freedom to co-create a better world.

I've been compelled to write this book for a number of
reasons—primarily because everything I've gone through
has led me to be called to serve others by sharing what I
know. Because of my experience, I feel that I'm meant to
help people retrieve something that exists in all of us but
has been collectively misplaced. I've found it, and I know
that you can, too, if you keep an open mind and are receptive to the unlimited possibilities of a life that includes your
intuition.

What I've Learned from All of You

I've had the immense privilege of sharing my gift of
intuitive insight, reading the lives of close to 20,000 individuals who have sought me out from 29 countries around
the world. Consequently, I've been exposed to the intimate

details of all kinds of people—from dog walkers, house-wives, and artists to doctors, politicians, and celebrities. I've learned from them (and from my own experiences), and as a result, I've come to several conclusions that are the basis for this book:

1. Intuition is the natural sixth sense bestowed upon everyone . . . *without exception.* It's akin to a radio with preset channels, and each of us was given one in the "how-to-be-a-human-being" package that we received at birth. We can tune in to something outside of our self-centered five-sensory perception of ourselves, receiving information through the sixth sense of intuition—our inner radio.

2. The power to receive information varies from person to person for a number of reasons that will be discussed later in these pages. Nonetheless, it's a natural ability that can be developed by *anyone* who tries. There's nothing complicated about it.

3. When we access our intuition, we're in contact with an inherent, limitless connection that defies the confines of modern thought and challenges our idea of reality. We have an unrestricted, natural link to the cosmos. Put another way, the perception of there being impermeable boundaries within what we can sense through sight, sound, taste, touch, and smell is an illusion. Through our intuition, we tune in to and access a much greater universe than our localized idea of the world, implying that *separation itself is an illusory device.*

4. Personal reality is limited by the perception of the ego-self (defined by the pronoun *Me*) that views itself as separate from others and from the Divine. I refer to this throughout this book as the "*Me* bubble," which is dependent on the illusion of separation in order to survive. If the ego-self loses its distinct identity—replacing it with a unified sense of the collective—it basically disappears. It is therefore invested in separation, and intuition is the natural ability to access the opposite: *connection*. Thus, the ego-self is intuition's enemy.

5. The reality outside our "bubbles" can also permeate and inform them. However, because these dual worlds don't obey the same laws of time and space, this clash may threaten our concept of a five-sensory reality, making us react with confusion and suspicion.

6. We're naturally and intrinsically connected to everything and everyone. Although a healthy sense of independence and uniqueness is important, the truth of our spiritual natures is that there are no borders to divide us. The consequence of this revelation is that ultimately, we're responsible for each other. This concept, therefore, also challenges all divisive scarcity activity based on the notion of "us against them." We're part of a living system—a unified collective where we continuously impact all of life through every thought, word, and action.

One of the most powerful truths that life has taught me is that our personal and collective experience is vastly greater than what we perceive it to be. In other words, there's a more profound way to understand our lives than the majority of us are even aware of.

I've seen this firsthand in my own life . . . I've lived it. Events and situations that weren't always of my own choosing have shown me that there's a spiritual lens that the world can be viewed through with absolute clarity. I've had astounding experiences that have absolutely proven to me that there's a spiritual world—another dimension of reality that's not local to our limited sense of self and identity. This is the place where our sixth sense takes us.

I've spent the last 20 years searching for explanations of what appears to be a phenomenon that's common to many individuals around the world. Given my own experience with intuition, and those of thousands of ordinary people who have confided in me about theirs, I'd say that it's actually *more* common for us to have daily intuitive experiences than not. Most people just don't know what to do with them and can't fathom their implications.

I didn't always understand these things either. I've struggled with the fear that I'd be deemed unacceptable by normal societal standards and be shunned . . . or worse, persecuted. I viewed my intuition as a swarm of buzzing flies surrounding me at all times, and I spent so much time shooing them away, thinking, *Go away! Leave me alone—this can't be right!*

In accordance with mainstream values, I was taught to prize intellect, rational thought, and modernity; discount magic as trickery; and derive my understanding through the empirical world. Only things that were measurable and provable through hard science were to be believed. There was nothing to help me explain the natural access I had to my intuitive abilities, because discussions of intuition, hearing voices, seeing visions, and having prescient dreams clearly aren't part of the acceptable paradigm.

All in the Family

The reality of my life experience, however, is that these strange powers are part of me, no matter how many times I've tried to avoid or deny them. And it's not as if they came out of nowhere: My father also had these gifts, although he was forced to repress them.

As a child, I received lots of mixed messages about intuition and spiritual phenomena. At home I was allowed to be relatively curious about these things, but I was absolutely discouraged from owning them—especially if they might interfere with my parents' aspirations for me to become a lawyer. Then again, my family was also trying to protect me from the negative social fallout that happens when one walks too far out on the fringe.

Those of us who devote our lives to the service of others by using our intuitive gift as our professions are still outside the mainstream today. Although the contemporary movement known as the "New Age" has afforded us a greater level of popularity in society, we're nevertheless lacking in widespread formal acceptance. However, there's a sign of growing interest, understanding, and curiosity in the spiritual/psychic world—this can be seen in the success of television shows such as *Medium* and *Ghost Whisperer,* in movies including *The Sixth Sense,* and in books by best-selling author and psychic Sylvia Browne. I suspect that the reason this is so is because people really do know that each one of us is essentially spirit in human form, and that even things that can't be explained empirically are still very real.

The Journey Ahead: Recovering Your Intuition

Intuition is the link to our soul's inner wisdom, but it can be blocked by unresolved emotional and psychological baggage. Therefore, just because we all have this gift, it doesn't mean that everyone has spiritual clarity. Some people still see the world through foggy lenses.

I discovered this in my own life. When I engaged in a conscious spiritual cleanup based on the seven principles outlined in this book—*truth, reverence, humility, courage, forgiveness, stillness,* and *love*—the door to the miracle of my soul's gift swung wide open. I believe that before you can engage your own intuition, you must clear the ego debris blocking your spirit from shining through. In essence, this book is about that very thing: a spiritual awakening that will lead you to effortlessly retrieve your own personal gift.

Recently I shared the stage with Sylvia Browne, who summed up my sentiments perfectly in her no-nonsense way. She said, "The more spiritual you are, the more psychic you will become." Clearly, you can't be psychically tuned *in* if you're spiritually tuned *out.* When you begin to incorporate the seven principles into your life each day, the awakening that will organically result is undeniable. You'll uncover your own unfailing relationship to your intuition as you navigate the world.

Although the exercises included in Part II of the book will help you develop your innate abilities, the intent of this work isn't to teach you how to become an "intuitive."

Rather, it's to assist you in recovering the right *relationship* to your sixth sense—to tune in to its voice and guidance. And whether you use it on behalf of others or just for yourself, the choice to embrace or ignore it lies in your own hands. Choose well!

I believe that once we learn how to access our intuition, our lives can be enriched beyond measure. By tapping in to this lost resource, everyday experiences can have the grace of deeper meaning. We can consciously co-create lives of our own choosing with the Divine, learning to respond with serenity and strength. Regardless of our emotional difficulties or past reactions to challenges, we can experience the magic of synchronicity and the completeness that comes from using all of our Divine gifts.

Recovering your intuition is a path that belongs to an ancient sacredness, a secret society in which we're all members. It's about the yearning for connection that meets itself in a magical mirror and says, "Yes, *I am.*" Recovering intuition reminds us that the soul doesn't live inside the body. I believe we live *inside the soul.* And this is how we're all united as spiritual beings in this human play on the stage of the natural world—ashes to ashes, dust to dust . . . windswept on the breath of God.

≫≪ ≫≪ ≫≪

PART I

MY STORY

Chapter 1

FROM THE BEGINNING: THE MOON, DREAMS, AND ME

Whenever I contemplate the moon, such as the way it illuminates the night sky and sheds light on the shadows in the world, I think about intuition and how it acts similarly, guiding me in the dark.

I'm actually ruled by the moon, as it's the celestial body that governs my astrological sign of Cancer. Its power to move the waters of the world and its obvious pull on humanity makes it seem like a mystical creature. Without it, none of us could navigate in the dark or experience the ebb and flow of nature . . . and I've never thought that it was made of cheese!

My mother was the first one to recognize that the moon had a big effect on me. From the time I was two years old until the ripe old age of four, the full moon would call to me when I was asleep, and my parents would suffer a monthly night without rest. My mom would find me sleep-walking in the hallway, jabbering away to some invisible friend—I did a lot of loud giggling with my imaginary pal.

My mom insisted that this incident happened only once a month and always on a full moon.

Baby Games and Hearing Voices

I first became aware that I was hearing voices when I was about four. It started with my mother's utterances, which I'd catch when I did something while she wasn't looking—her exact reaction and response was recited verbatim in my mind. I'd wait for her to notice whatever I'd done, and when she did, it was amazing to me that she would repeat (in the same tone) exactly what I'd heard inside my head only minutes before.

My mom told me that I'd play games with her in this manner when I was even younger: still in a high chair with a bib. As soon as she turned her back during dinner, I'd take my bowl of Jell-O, creamed spinach, or spaghetti with lots of sauce and promptly dump it on my head. There I'd be with a silly grin on my little face—goop dripping down my head, cheeks, and all over the floor—while I gurgled with delight at the show that was about to begin. My mother told me that she was convinced I was waiting for her to respond in a very specific manner, because I watched and listened to her so intently, laughing my head off in my high chair when I finally got the reaction I was looking for. She said I was a really weird kid.

Ever since I can remember, I've known things in advance. Sometimes they were mundane, and on other occasions, they were weightier images about the future. For example, I always knew exactly *how* my mother was going to yell at me, or the fact that my father would forget to buy the tuna before coming home. And I knew the gist of conversations that transpired between my parents at the breakfast table days before they occurred.

I used to sit and play with my Barbie and Ken dolls, pretending that they were my parents. I'd remember a discussion that I thought I'd heard between them, and my dolls would act it out. A few days afterward (or sometimes mere hours later), the scene would unfold between my mom and dad exactly as I'd "remembered" it, which always entertained me, but it also confused me a little.

Sometimes I was aware of simple things, such as when my favorite chocolate cake with the green sprinkles would be made at the bakery . . . a day before it was. But then there was the time when I knew that the owner was going to die that coming autumn. The previous summer I remember telling my mom that I was going to miss the baker, and that we should stock up on the cake because it wouldn't be made the same way by anyone other than him. She had no idea what I was talking about and refused to buy more of the dessert—which really upset me, as I was so sure that I was right and no one wanted to listen to me.

I didn't think that there was anything "different" about the things that I knew, because my premonitions occurred frequently and seemed perfectly normal to me. So it confused me when I was told to be quiet all the time. I was "remembering" things that hadn't happened yet, but I didn't know the difference. And I got the same reaction when I would pick up private information about my mother's friends.

On one occasion, I was severely punished and sent to my room without my stuffed monkey when I blurted out the name of the man whom one of my mom's friends was seeing. I kept hearing his name in my head: *Paul, Paul, Paul, Paul.* I knew that he'd gone away, so I looked at the lady and said, "Don't be sad that Paul is gone. . . . He's coming back—he fell in the toilet."

Without warning, my mother stood up, smacked my bottom, and sent me upstairs. She was so angry that she scolded me, "Never open your mouth in front of guests again!" I didn't find out until 25 years later that my mom had punished me because she thought that I'd overheard and repeated a telephone conversation that she'd had with her friend the day before. It turns out that Paul was a plumber, and apparently her friend had called him a piece of shit! Shortly after sending me to my room, my mother realized that I couldn't have overheard them, as I'd been at nursery school when the incident originally occurred—but I still had to stay up there.

So that was my early life and how it all began. There was no invisible fence, no line that I knew of to cross . . . at times I was just able to see and experience the world from a different vantage point in time. It wasn't until much later, when I realized that not everybody had these experiences, that I began to withdraw and try to escape.

Family Secrets and the Intrusion of Dreams

I had recurring nightmares from the age of three until about five. They were identical every time: Again and again, I'd dream about fires and clouds of ash, silver balloons dropping explosives on a ravaged city, an emaciated man burning in a giant oven, and another skinny man crying while removing metal from broken teeth on a table. I remember those images vividly because they were accompanied by a horrible stench that I've never smelled while awake, but I've heard it described as the odor of death.

It turns out that these dreams also happened around the full moon, which explains why there was always so much tension in my family surrounding my relationship to it. When I'd wake up crying and tell my mother about the details of my nightmare, she always had the same panicked look on her face that I never understood. I had no idea why she couldn't comfort me, why she didn't want to hold me or pick me up. It was as though the images that I described produced a terrified reaction in her as well, but I didn't comprehend how this could be.

Of course, at the time that I was having those terrible dreams, I was unaware of the legacy of the Holocaust. I didn't know that the ravages of World War II had taken an enormous toll on both my parents: Each of them was a European who'd fled to Canada to escape the past and leave behind the painful things that he or she had witnessed. I found out much later that my mother struggled with her memories of the Holocaust, and that my nightmares were not just dreams, but images of real events that she'd experienced in Berlin during the war. (My grandfather, who was killed in the concentration camp at Dachau, may very well have been the man in my dreams.)

These were my mother's secrets, however, and although she didn't share them with me as a tiny child, they were revealed to me while I slept. The silver balloons that I saw were zeppelins and planes dropping bombs on her city, and the teeth on the table were from the people who'd died in the camps—the gold from their fillings was removed for barter and often made into trinkets for the wives of the SS officers.

For the first 20 years or so of my life, I was raised as a Christian and never knew that I came from Jewish ancestry. Yet on the full-moon nights when I sometimes experienced those terrifying images—instead of the make-believe giggling conversations I had with my imaginary friends—I saw over and over what had happened to my relatives.

⇒⇐ ⇒⇐ ⇒⇐

Chapter 2

EARLY INTUITIVE MEMORIES—
GROWING UP "DIFFERENT"

From the time that I was four years old, my sister and I attended a private Anglican school for girls in Toronto that was known to be "reserved" for the upper-class, WASPy, old-moneyed young ladies of society. (However, at that time it was beginning to open its doors to *any* girl from a reasonably suitable family who could pay.)

I grew up in that place. In fact, we all wore the exact same uniform from our nursery days through the end of high school. And although there were some wonderful times, I remember feeling marginalized by a few of the teachers who consistently reminded me that my parents weren't real "Canadians," and therefore we didn't really belong in the social circles we moved in. I felt tolerated, rather than included, by some of the older faculty members during most of my time at school.

One of my most vivid memories from these years is of my mother's lovely German marble cakes, which remained unsold at the bake sales at school and at our church. I remember overhearing someone say that it was because they were "foreign." I never forgot that.

God Bless the Nanny

I dealt with feelings of not fitting in throughout most of my childhood. It was a confusing time in my life until I was given a wonderful gift in the form of our Scottish nanny, Mrs. Kelly. She was in her 70s when she was hired to help my mother take care of us. Besides being a wonderful caretaker, Mrs. Kelly was also a bona fide psychic. When my mom wasn't home, she'd sit at our kitchen table with her playing cards, mesmerizing us with her stories about our future, as well as anyone else's who came to visit.

I remember her well—she was a strange and eccentric old woman, an avid gambler who smelled of lavender and violets and who croaked like a frog as she spoke in her heavy Scottish brogue . . . and I loved her with all my heart. She was sure that her sixth sense was the reason she won at the racetrack so frequently. She told me that spirits spoke to her there for the sole purpose of divulging the names of winning horses. She lived a full life and enjoyed it all: babysitting, chatting with the dead, and betting on the ponies.

Mrs. Kelly was very open about her psychic talents and always had stories to tell us about the spirit world. She also made it very clear that I had the gift as well. Although she'd modify her words when she described what she saw so that they'd make sense to a child, she seemed to sense my destiny long before I found my path on my own. She used to say things such as, "You know, dearie, the tunnel will be long, but even when terrible things happen, I see that the angels will catch you. You might find yourself in a stormy sea, but you won't drown. No, you won't drown—I see that. You'll always have it: the *Sight,* you know . . . the *Sight!"*

Of course, *I* only wanted to know when Prince Charming would come, and whether I'd get married at 18, have six kids, and be rich. However, she seemed to want to talk about other more serious things, and I remember her concern for me as a child. Long before I took my first sip of alcohol, she used to warn me, "You must beware the drink, dearie. Beware the drink!"

I had no idea what she meant at the time. I assumed that she was talking about the yucky-tasting juice that my mother brought home from the German market. It's interesting for me to reflect back on her words years later, after battling alcoholism; at the same time, it's comforting to know that she also saw that I'd make something of myself in spite of my problems.

As Mrs. Kelly knew, I did have the gift of Sight. When I started to ask her questions about why I saw lights around everybody's head that no one else seemed to see, she explained auras to me. I told her that my mom would punish me when I asked her if I was seeing fairies in the backyard, and my nanny would laugh, reassuring me that that was absolutely what I was observing.

I always saw these beings out of the corner of my eye. They were creatures that resembled dragonflies with humanlike features, and they seemed to communicate with me—but as soon as I'd try to look at them directly, they'd vanish. I always knew that fairies existed, though, regardless of what others might say. Mrs. Kelly helped me realize that they were real and not just figments of my imagination.

When I told her about the lights that I saw around people pretty much all the time, she confirmed that I was seeing their spirits and the energy of their souls. However, she warned that it would be best if I kept this knowledge to myself. One day in particular, I clearly remember hearing her tell my mother that I had the gift of Sight, and Mom asked her to keep her voice down, as if it were a big secret.

At the time, I couldn't understand what all the whispering was about. I thought Mrs. Kelly was trying to tell my mother that I'd never have to wear glasses like the rest of my family. I recall feeling so relieved, as I was vain enough to know that I'd be more attractive without glasses. Since I didn't think that I was all that pretty to begin with, I knew that I needed to make the most of what I had—being able to see unaided was hugely reassuring. As I matured, I came to realize that my mom and Mrs. Kelly hadn't been discussing my eyesight after all. But I still didn't understand why my intuitive gifts had to be such a big secret, or why my mother was so unhappy about them.

I'm sure that this negative response to my abilities contributed to the feelings of anxiety and rejection that I experienced while growing up. I always had the impression of being emotionally and psychologically overwhelmed, forever struggling to fit in and never feeling as if I belonged anywhere. I felt inundated with information all the time, as though the world were just too loud and was swallowing me up. I felt restless and dissociated from reality, as if I were behind a window, looking out at the universe with my hands pressed against the glass. I could always watch, but I'd never truly be a part of the life on the other side.

There was one location, however, where I didn't feel like an outsider locked behind the glass. That place was church.

Holy Halos! Whose God Is It?

When I went to church, the stained-glass windows and depictions of Christian mythology enthralled me. I loved seeing portrayals of the saints—to me their halos meant that everyone was holy, because the lights that I saw around their heads were the same ones I observed around everybody, and that amazed me. I associated spirituality with this visual phenomenon.

I loved everything and everyone associated with my new world in the church: Jesus, Mary, Joseph, Noah, the 12 apostles, the Ten Commandments, the seven deadly sins, the Holy Ghost, and heaven. And I especially loved the music, equating it with God. Even though I had no idea what I was singing about, I had the greatest feeling while doing it: It was an intuitive knowing that with God, I was whole. When I sat in those church pews, hymnal in hand, I felt that I fit in and was heard. There I could be part of a harmony that needed different notes—all of them just as important together as they were individually. I finally felt as though I belonged somewhere.

As much as I fell in love with God in church, my personal experiences with religion were complicated. My first realization that it could be a means of separating people instead of bringing them together happened in the third grade. My parents didn't want me to be instructed by the teacher at the school I was attending, so they decided to temporarily pull me out of it and place me in a Catholic one.

I was one of maybe three non-Catholic girls in the class. The nuns fascinated me, and I loved the school. I enjoyed going to the chapel, where the services were filled with rituals and beautiful rosaries. The bottom line was that I adored being a pretend Catholic. My school inspired me, and I was even voted vice president of my class.

It was all great until the day I learned a very important lesson when the class president stayed home sick. She always led the prayer service in chapel, and her duties fell to the vice president in case of absence. I was very excited and so proud that I was going to be allowed this honor.

I proudly marched into the chapel and stood beneath the beautiful carved Christ and the dome of sparkling stained glass, ready to begin the prayers. Closing my eyes and clasping my hands very solemnly, I opened my mouth and started to recite. Immediately, I was swarmed by two nuns, who pulled at my arms and yanked me from the lectern. They sternly and loudly told me that I was never allowed to lead the prayers because I wasn't Catholic, and they ordered me to sit down. I was so overwhelmed with shame that I started to cry—but I quickly pulled myself together, even as the other little girls glared at me.

The behavior I was witnessing went against every fiber of my being, and the intuitive warning bells in my head clanged loudly. I sat there thinking, *How can they have a different Jesus than I do? How is it that they can pray to him and I can't? Am I not good enough? We have the same God, and I'm a Christian.* I just didn't get it.

I went home and told my mom what happened. I cried and cried, revealing to her that I had a secret longing to become a nun, so the incident was especially sad for me. I can only imagine what my mother must have been feeling when she heard me tell her all this, since she was hiding the fact that we were Jewish. Needless to say, I was taken out of that school faster than I could say "Julie Andrews." You can imagine how weird it was for me to find out later on what my real heritage was.

These experiences all had a profound influence on my feelings about religion and are the reason why I'm so committed to spiritual unity and harmony in my work today. I saw so much confusion and suffering in my own life in the name of God. What was born of these early experiences was a certainty that there's a halo around every person's head on the planet—that we're all equally holy—and I will die believing that. I learned through a little bit of sadness and bewilderment that it isn't God Who divides us—human beings are the ones who cause all the separation and sorrow in the world.

Dominica and the Flying Saucers

My family and I lived in the West Indies for a short time when I was about eight years old. My father was working on a land-development deal in Dominica, a volcanic island with black sand that would scorch our feet at midday before the skies opened up to pour down buckets of torrential rain for two hours each afternoon.

It was a miraculous period for me. For the first time, I clearly saw that plants and animals could also glow with the same halos that people did. It was in the jungle that I began to understand the connection between God and nature. I spent my days collecting lizards; playing with two goats; and carrying around my frog, Charlie. (My pet was a species that was uncommonly large and frequently eaten—the natives called it a "mountain chicken.")

Dominica was a strange and magical place—when we lived there, it was sparsely populated except for a couple of towns (that I can remember), Mero and Roseau. There were only two hotels on the island: one at the top near the volcano, and another at the bottom by the beach, which was close to our house. The lure of the island was that it was still relatively undeveloped—a gold mine for real estate investors.

The appeal to my father, aside from these opportunities, was something unexpected that I found absolutely fascinating. In the middle of the night, he'd sometimes pull my sister and me out of bed and hurry us onto the veranda. There we'd sit, bundled in our blankets and surrounded by jungle blackness, watching bright lights fly across the sky. He told us that they were UFOs.

I remember that there were always seven of them flying in unison. These incredibly brilliant, oblong lights would zoom swiftly in one direction and then suddenly split up and hover in another place. I recall my father telling us that we needed to always remember that we weren't alone in the universe, and that one day everybody would come to know this.

We saw these flying saucers at least 20 times while on the island. Once when we were on a boat at sundown, my dad said that he witnessed a UFO fly from the sky into one of the nearby bat caves. Unfortunately, I missed seeing this because just as he excitedly pointed it out, a giant manta ray leapt out of the ocean, blocking out the sun and causing me to turn away in fright.

I came to look forward to the quiet midnight escapades with the UFOs, so I was terribly disappointed on the nights when the boats would come in—in addition to being a haven for UFOs (as my dad used to say), Dominica was also a popular stopover for French yachts. When this happened, I knew that there would be no late-night rendezvous with my father. Although it may be hard to believe, the yachtsmen would moor their ships outside the many bat caves that peppered the coastline and bring their small boats to shore in order to have orgies on the beach—directly in front of our house.

When the boats came in, my mother would lock us in our rooms and play music loudly to mask the noise. If my sister or I asked what was going on, she became agitated with us and explained that there was "bad dancing on the beach" and going near it was forbidden. I never saw anything, but I certainly heard a lot of laughter and screaming. Shut up in my room for the duration of the night, I'd lie in bed and wonder if the UFOs were watching, and what they thought about the beach parties. If it looked anything like it sounded, I imagined that the aliens must have thought we humans were pretty wild!

What I remember most about my time in Dominica was that I was aware of the constant whispers of the "other side" emanating from the jungle. Interestingly enough, my father never disputed my claims that the forest was alive with spirits. In fact, if I told him about them when he and I were alone, this was the only time I can recall him agreeing with me and not shooing me away or telling me that I should do my homework.

When we were by ourselves and my mother wasn't there to show her fear and disapproval, I was able to witness my dad's true feelings. Nonetheless, my gift of Sight was never to be an acceptable or encouraged ability once we got back to Canada and away from this strange paradise, with its jungle ghosts and UFOs that flew into bat caves.

Scandal in the Coffee Grounds

I later learned why my father could talk to me about those spirits in the jungle: He was the one in our family with the strongest intuitive abilities, and it's possible that my personal gifts came to me through him. One of his oldest friends recently told me the following story about him.

When I was about three years old, whenever my dad would attend a party he'd look at the remains left behind in the guests' Turkish coffee cups at the end of the evening. My father could see things by staring into the grounds at the bottom of the cup. This is actually a form of divination called "tasseomancy," which usually refers to reading tea leaves, although Dad practiced it with coffee grounds.

He was very good at this and apparently went into trances in which he revealed very telling and private things about the guests. Naturally, this made him the life of the party—and it was all well and good until the night my father pointed out the affair one woman was having with another guest's husband. Like the time that I was sent to my room for "remembering" the private conversation between my mother and her friend, Mom promptly forbade my father to "see" for anyone ever again.

So—gag order firmly in place—this family trait was only brought up in the most oblique way and with a sort of disdain, if it was mentioned at all. Whenever I tried to talk to my mother about anything related to the spirit world, she'd disregard what I was saying (although I found out years later that she secretly loved to go to psychics, so perhaps at the time she just didn't want her daughter to be one).

Strangely enough, in the last year of her life, my mom told me that she was proud of me for becoming an intuitive. However, I can think of a time when one of my dad's associates asked me what I did for a living, and my mother interrupted before I could open my mouth, loudly declaring: "She's in marketing!"

≫≪ ≫≪ ≫≪

Chapter 3

THE TEEN YEARS—
ESCAPE FROM THE GIFT

As I entered my teens, I was unable to cope with the sensitivity that continued to develop within me. In fact, to this day I very clearly remember a few incidents that had a strong impact on me.

My girlfriend's father was a lawyer, and when I visited her house I saw what appeared to be his driver's license on the floor. But when I stooped to pick it up, it would disappear . . . and this happened on three consecutive visits. I never said anything about it, since seeing things that weren't there wasn't new for me. Then a few years later, after they'd moved to another city, I found out that my friend's father had been charged with fraud and had lost his license to practice law.

Another time I was visiting a different girlfriend's family farm for a sleepover. I was sick with fear and felt horrible whenever I passed her brother's bedroom. Each time I walked by his door, I felt someone pull my hair—but when I turned around, no one was there. Later I was told in confidence that he had repeatedly molested my friend for many years, and that the abuse had mostly happened at the farm.

Those were the last two intuitive events that I can remember before my abilities left me for a time. Other things began filling my mind as my parents guided me toward a future that they felt was in my best interest. My mom and dad had the mind-set that academia was every-thing—that money could make you safe, a good educa-tion was an insurance policy, and fitting in was essential. Logic and reason were absolute, and appearances spoke volumes.

My father and mother had emigrated to Canada to start a new life. My dad had even changed our last name to accommodate the need to be upwardly mobile and more socially acceptable. So we went from "Bogdanovic" to "Baron." Dad had done this because nobody could pro-nounce Bogdanovic, but he also enjoyed the aristocratic flair that Baron suggested, which implied that we were titled. I think that's why my sister and I were accepted into private school—the administration thought we were nobil-ity. I did nothing to discourage that belief; as a matter of fact, I chose to maintain the fantasy myself.

Because I was getting older, school became the main focus of my life. I was being groomed for the future my parents had envisioned for me, and they did everything in their power to ensure that all would go according to plan. But in the end, they couldn't control me, and I spent my teens rebelling against everything and everybody.

I felt constrained by my parents' good intentions. They were very strict, and I *was* a teenager during the cultural revolutions of the 1960s and early '70s. During that time, I could no longer deal with the intuitive information I was picking up—it all seemed to blend together and ended up overwhelming me. It was like a loud drone of sound that didn't belong to me, so I tried to find ways to escape it.

The only occasion when I felt okay about myself and safe in my own head for any length of time was when I was listening to music, playing guitar, or singing. I could move my mind into the same place where I heard and saw my intuitive information. There I was able to experience the bounty, expansiveness, and beauty of the melodies without the mental cacophony of voices and visions that always seemed to relate to everybody else and never me. So it was initially through music that I was able to take control of my intuitive abilities and make them more manageable.

Unfortunately, my parents saw my interest in popular music as a disaster in the making. They made me learn classical guitar so I'd play in a style that they felt was more suitable. Yet I hated my teacher, who had bad breath and pasty-white fingers. I felt too aware of him: He was much more conscious of *me* than he should have been, and it made me uncomfortable.

I was also uninterested in the classical craft. Folk and modern popular music inspired me, and soon I began to write songs on my own, teaching myself by listening to Joni Mitchell records and playing along. Music was becoming my savior, my place of redemption. I learned that I could pull compositions out of the air in the same way that I could draw upon my visions. But when the music wasn't there to buffer me, I still had an acute sensitivity to the outside world. Coupled with my teenage rebellion, this brewed a toxic mixture of fear and anger within me. In an effort to find a safe place in my mind, I began to seek out other ways of coping.

My first response was to become bulimic. I was so full of rage and confusion that at the age of 15, I began to eat compulsively and then vomit. This was a part of my life that troubled me off and on for many years. My eating disorders pushed my sensitivity away, but the hiding places they provided were always only temporary. Rebellious to the core, I began hanging around the kids at school who smoked cigarettes, drank, and did drugs. With them I found another temporary panacea: alcohol.

I had my first drink when I was 12, and I immediately liked it. (We always had alcohol in our home, as was common in many European households.) At 15, however, I started to abuse it. I now realize that I had no control over this substance from the day I took my first sip—I was powerless but in total denial. When I started drinking, I couldn't stop. However, the blackouts, while confusing, were also great escapes for me. Plus, I thought they were cool, and that's what I wanted to be more than anything else in the world.

Drinking worked in the beginning: I felt wonderful, warm, and fuzzy . . . almost pretty. Most important, for a while I even stopped hearing the voices in my head. I no longer saw visions either, and they were gone for the next four years, becoming just a faded memory as I sat around writing music, going to school, and planning my escape.

What I didn't know was that I was in a prison of my own making, and I was the only one who could hold the key—but unfortunately, I'd already lost it. For the next few years, I acted out in self-destructive ways, causing a tremendous amount of pain to my family. During that time, I forgot about God and the people who loved me and started thinking only about myself.

≫≪ ≫≪ ≫≪

Chapter 4

SURRENDER

The event that was most pivotal in returning my gift to me was a situation that was to change me forever. I was 19 years old, and my alcoholism had progressed along with my self-centeredness—I was frozen in immaturity. I was managing my eating disorder by taking diet pills and drinking to temper their effects. By this time, I was also using street drugs on top of everything else. I was screaming inside for help, but none came.

After taking an overdose the day before final exams as a pre-law freshman in college, I went to summer school to make up for the year that I'd sabotaged. I was depressed and didn't know what to do: My intuition was blocked and muffled by all the poison I was taking into my body, and my destructiveness made it impossible to hear the warnings of my soul.

My friends on campus cautioned me to stay away from a particular bar in a seedy part of town that was rumored to attract a wilder kind of crowd. Of course, that just intrigued me more, so I went there with a friend and started hanging around. Needless to say, as a young, rebellious, curious, and self-destructive girl who was desperate for attention and not very experienced with men, I got into trouble. The place was frequented by all kinds of rough guys—drug dealers and bikers among them. I should have known better, but I'd never been exposed to this element of society before, except in the form of romanticized novels and movies.

My first taste of the dangers of that scene came one night after I insulted one of the men in front of his gang of friends. For the first time in my life, I received a violent beating at the hands of a man. His fist hit my face full on, and I flew backward over a chair and landed on the floor. I heard a crack and a hollow thud, and I must have passed out for a few seconds.

I remember picking myself up off the floor . . . the room was spinning, I could taste the blood running into my mouth, and both the front and back of my head were pounding. I'd never been hit before—I was shocked, humiliated, and very scared. No one helped me up from the floor. I'd apparently done the unthinkable, although I wasn't exactly sure what that was. . . . However, it was what happened two weeks later that would change my life forever.

I was beginning to feel cooped up in my school's dorm, where I'd remained since the incident at the bar. Still shocked by my experience, and with the bruise still evident on my face, I let my girlfriend convince me to go downtown for a beer. Later that evening we ran into a group of guys we'd seen around. I was ready to go home, but my friend wanted to stay longer, so I accepted a lift from the men. I didn't know them very well, but they seemed nice, and they'd never bothered me before.

After what had occurred two weeks earlier, I was looking for protection, so I believed them when they offered to get me home safely. Little did I know that these men had other plans for me—an experience that showed me what it was like to lose the power to choose what would happen to my own body, as well as making me truly understand the nature of shame. But the situation would also open the door to those abilities that I had previously pushed away.

The interesting thing was that the minute I accepted the ride, I knew something terrible was going to happen, but I just wasn't able to listen. My intuition was there to show me the way, but I was drunk and couldn't hear it. Although a sense of fearful expectation made my heart race, I hoped that what I anticipated was just my imagination . . . but it turned out to be all too real. Something important was indeed about to take place: I was going to be raped.

As these men violated me, I had an extraordinary and unforgettable experience. I remember it vividly, as if it were only yesterday. I saw myself being lifted out of my body, floating up to the corner of the room. I looked down at the scene below, observing what was happening to me in a calm, detached, curious way. I remember feeling very old, as if I had been a soul since the beginning of time.

At the same time, my intuitive gift began to reveal scenes to me from the lives of my assailants. I started to feel oddly sorry for them. I saw a child locked in the basement without food and water, left there by his fat, slovenly, alcoholic mother. I witnessed another small and skinny boy being shuffled in and out of foster homes. A third one had pale white skin and red hair and was part of a large family—I heard yelling and screaming in a kitchen, and I saw the father beating the mother to the floor and the little boy seething with rage. Then I saw someone in a grocery store stealing cans of soup and placing them in a big, unfamiliar purse.

These images swirled around me and were suspended in the room. I also experienced a split awareness: I was conscious of myself, and at the same time, I was able to "walk" beside my own mind, jumping back and forth at will. Later in life, I recognized that this is exactly the same "location" that I'm able to visit when I read for people.

What happened to me that night left me with two distinct legacies: The first was the shameful wound of rape that took many years to heal; the second and more important one was the dual awareness that I experienced. From that day forward, I was able to access this awareness at will, and it ultimately became the key to my hunger to know and understand the vastness of human consciousness and perception. But this change for the better wasn't immediate.

Shame and Silence

For the next few years, I remained in situations that placed me in harm's way. I was confused, and I prayed to God but believed He would ignore me. And my mother made me promise never to tell anyone about my experience, as she herself was a gang-rape survivor. (During the war, she'd been assaulted by a group of Russian soldiers while her adopted father was forced to watch.)

I'd never wanted anyone to know about the rape. I kept it to myself until I collapsed a month later, hemorrhaging, with a super-high temperature. During my subsequent stay in the hospital, I revealed the truth to my shattered parents. I was also told at the age of 19 that I'd likely never be able to bear children.

It took nine more years for me to hit bottom. The alcohol and drugs no longer provided escapes from my intuitive abilities, although the messages and visions were distorted and filtered through my damaged ego. I wore the perception of myself as a victim like a badge and made it—and my shame—the excuse for self-destruction.

I got involved in relationships with men that mirrored the abuse I'd come to expect, and I hung out with a wild group of people who partied all the time. My life became about going to clubs; staying up all night; working in bars, telemarketing offices, and retail clothing stores; and trying to make it as a singer/songwriter. However, I was failing at everything I touched. I had odd and obvious intuitive experiences that were undeniable, but I pushed them away and called them hallucinations. And I thought about suicide every day.

My intuitive gift became increasingly difficult to suppress, so I stopped trying. With twenty-twenty hindsight, of course, I see that I had a strong six-sensory perspective on the people around me, what they were going through, and what was about to happen. But because I was never sober, I was unable to put this to good use.

Stolen Passports: Seeing Under Carpets

One night at a party I overheard two men talking about the fact that they'd lost their passports. One of the guys had placed them in a hiding place, but when they went back to get them, they were gone. In a flash, I saw exactly who had stolen them and where they were stashed.

In my mind, I observed a Persian carpet, and looking right through it, I could "see" the passports—one of them with money in it. The next day I went to another party with my best friend at the time. While the house we were visiting was unknown to me, I immediately knew that it was the same place where the passports were hidden.

When I was introduced to the man who was hosting the party, I recognized him . . . even though I'd never met him before. Later in the evening while searching for the bathroom, I found myself in a room, where—looking down at the floor—I saw the exact carpet that I'd previously envisioned. I quickly lifted it up and found the passports, promptly gathered the stolen items, and went to let my girlfriend know what I'd found. I told her that we should give them back to their rightful owners, but she convinced me that it was none of our business. She explained that we should leave the party and never tell anyone about what I'd found in case no one believed us—because it all seemed too weird to be true.

I put the passports back, and we left the house. Yet I was bothered by my conscience afterward. I believed that I'd seen these things for the good of someone else, and I felt guilty that I hadn't returned the stolen items. My friend teased me after that by calling me "411," and she'd often tell people, "Need to know something? Go ask spooky Colette."

Around the same time, one of my pals was very much interested in tarot cards, and although she wasn't particularly intuitive, she was obsessed with reading them for herself and the people around her. I went over some of her books that dealt with the subject of connecting to the soul through objects, omens, and ritual, as well as the history of divination in different cultures. Those works spoke to me at a really deep level because I recognized the capability they described in myself.

Another friend who was a lot older than I and was also into tarot cards bought me my first deck. I never really learned to read the cards by the book; rather, I found a way to decipher their symbols intuitively to confirm circumstances that I saw in my mind's eye. (Professionally, I still find them to be a useful tool in sessions.)

One of the cards in particular interested me more than the others—not surprisingly, it was called the Moon. Today, I recognize it as the archetype and symbol of the unseen forces in human beings and the world. The Moon is an image that represents the stirrings of the unconscious. In traditional tarot readings, it positively represents a psychic awakening that can enrich one's life, or negatively, the mystery of addiction and the consequences of a disturbed psyche. So through the tarot, the Moon and I continued our familiar and strangely compelling relationship.

My interest in tarot cards was a constant source of entertainment for myself and others, but creating music was still my priority. It was the only connection I had to something that allowed me to express myself fully, and this period was a time of prolific songwriting for me. Angst is a great fuel for poetry, and I vibrated musically to what I perceived as the deep chord of suffering in the world. It was the early '80s, and there was a lot of great music around to inspire me.

I saw myself as the wounded songstress—a secret contestant in the "Miss Victim of the World Pageant," and these feelings informed what I created. In my search for a false sense of affirmation from the world, there was something undeniable in my music that even I couldn't destroy. I used to joke about being a rock star and "making it big," but secretly I thought that success in the music business would make me a whole person, and that the accolades I dreamed of would wash away all the dirt that I believed was still stuck to me.

I'm so grateful today that nothing substantial actually happened with my career at that time because I would have become a casualty—no question about it. I don't think that I could have handled the truth: The applause and the money would have done nothing to change me. I would have overdosed, or in my selfishness, committed suicide. I'm sure of that, because between the ages of 20 and 22, I tried more than once.

I knew that I was in trouble with my substance abuse long before I could stop—before I even wanted to. By the time I was 22, I was afraid of myself and my experiences. Fueled by alcohol and the unresolved pain of my past, I continued down my self-destructive path. Then I found the fast track to hell and hit rock bottom when I started smoking cocaine (it wasn't called "crack" yet). I know firsthand what it's like to be insane and to lose your self-respect, morality, and basic sense of human decency to addiction. I should have died—I came close so many times—but God had other plans for me.

The Bottom and the Bubble

Just after Halloween in 1985, my family was devastated: We had to put our beloved dog to sleep because he had cancer and we couldn't pay for a vet. My father had lost everything at the age of 75, and we watched a few million dollars disappear virtually overnight, along with our house and—worst of all—my dad's pride and dignity. He sat for hours staring at nothing, smoking cigarettes, and suffering from the effects of numerous strokes and the onset of Alzheimer's, while my mother cried, terrified that what little money we had left wouldn't be enough to cover expenses.

I'll always remember the night I surrendered my life to God. I'd gone to see a dealer who was giving me drugs for "free." I walked up the stairs to the bathroom and looked at myself in the mirror. For the first time, I saw myself as I really was: demoralized, bankrupt in every way, and devoid of a sense of humanity. The whites of my eyes were yellow from jaundice, my skin was puckered from dehydration, my teeth were loose, and my gums bled. I saw sores all over my body that I'd somehow neglected to notice before—including large bruises that I couldn't even remember receiving.

I'd traded everything for my addiction, and I knew I was going to die. In that moment, I recited the first honest prayer I'd said in years, and I meant it with all my heart and soul. Shaking, I held the sides of the sink with my dirty hands and cried, "Help me!"

Some may say that what happened next was just a hallucination from the drugs, but I know differently. I saw an iridescent light around me in the mirror . . . it was as if I were encased in a bubble and everything around me looked clearer. I was calm, and I knew beyond a shadow of a doubt that it was over. I was certain that I would never set foot in that drug dealer's house again. I didn't understand how, but something profound was talking to me, telling me that I'd be all right and needed to surrender—and I listened and never went back.

≫≪ ≫≪ ≫≪

Chapter 5

THE BEGINNING OF GRACE

A series of miracles took place in rapid succession, and I was led to a facility for women in Toronto called the Jean Tweed Treatment Centre. It was really strange how in an instant of surrender, everything changed. It was just like the moment that the Red Sea parted for Moses—every obstacle was moved aside, and one by one, people arrived to support me as I began to find my way home.

Soon after that time, I met a woman at a party who was talkative and self-confident, and she engaged me in conversation about all things spiritual. I felt really comfortable with her, so I told her about the strange experiences I'd been having with my gift ever since I was a child. She shared a few of her own encounters with spiritual phenomena, and I was glad to chat with someone I could relate to. She told me in confidence that her grandmother had been a renowned psychic and healer, and that her family believed that intuitive abilities were passed down from mother to daughter. She informed me that she, too, could see auras, and that like me, she was able to read energy from objects.

Our psychic experiences differed somewhat in that she hadn't been as troubled by her ability as I had been by mine. Although I was greatly comforted, I convinced myself that in order to survive in the world, I needed to close down my intuitive side permanently. I wanted to fit in more than anything, and I wished that my past would just disappear.

I made a conscious decision to deny the part of myself that I came to see as dangerous and unwanted. This was all right for a time, and the next two years were like a pregnant pause, as if I were protecting something sacred that was yet to be born. I threw myself into getting well and developing a deeply committed spiritual life and practice. I began attending meetings in church basements with other recovering alcoholics and addicts who were helping each other and following spiritual principles to transform their lives. I was introduced to the concept of a Higher Power that could restore me to sanity if I placed my will and life in His care—the care of God.

I truly experienced a miracle, since I couldn't do this on my own. From that time on—since January 2, 1986—the compulsion to drink and use drugs completely lifted and has never returned. I've remained clean and sober ever since.

The God-Shaped Hole

I think that during my entire life I've had a God-shaped hole inside me, one that I used to try to fill with so many different things: men, alcohol, food, drugs, and shopping.

But with a spiritual life as the new center of my focus, this void was finally being filled with God. The old, lonely sense of the Divine as transcendent and outside of me somewhere "over there" was replaced by the knowledge that God is ever present and immanent, and He could be expressed through me. As I became more giving; completed good works; and acted with faith, forgiveness, and compassion, the universe showed me that it was possible for me to flourish.

Those two years were relatively peaceful for me personally. I was really happy for the first time in my life as I began to feel comfortable in my own skin. But as I improved, my family did the opposite: My father's health deteriorated further, and my mother—his primary caregiver—strained under the pressure. Both of my parents began to drink, and I watched them die slowly before me. I was powerless to do anything about it as I clung tenuously to my new life.

I focused on what appeared to be my promising musical career. I sang on various projects and then put together my own band, Isis (named after the Egyptian goddess). One of the women in the band gave me a book that had a strange effect on me. It was called *The Mists of Avalon,* and as I read it, I started remembering more of my intuitive gift. In the book, the symbol of a priestess who was initiated into the Temple of Isis was a blue moon tattooed on the forehead. And as I read about the priestesses and their training in Avalon, I experienced a strange memory: When I was little, I used to paint little blue crescent moons in the center of my forehead with ballpoint pen, ink, or finger paint. (There's that moon again!)

I loved that book, and I gobbled up more and more of the works that my friend recommended. I studied Seth, as well as the books of Shakti Gawain, Sanaya Roman, Elizabeth Clare Prophet, John Randolph Price, Ernest Holmes,

Helena Blavatsky, and Rudolf Steiner. As I read about the spiritualist movement at the turn of the century, I began to remember who I was. My band didn't last long, but my path became crystal clear, even though I still had a lot of ingrained resistance.

My First Mentor and the Return of the Visions

I believe that fate puts certain teammates together in the game of life, and then we all have the free will to play or not. Perhaps it's the karma of unfinished business from a past life that still needs to be resolved—all I know is that throughout my life, souls have been placed in front of me to accelerate my growth, and their appearance has left an indelible mark.

I was introduced to Yvonne when she arrived in Toronto from England. She was a well-regarded psychic-intuitive, and I went to her for a reading. In addition to accurately telling me much of what had already happened (a true sign of a good reading), she spotted my ability quickly and predicted many things that were to come.

She was also giving certification classes in holistic aroma-therapy, and I studied various alternative-healing techniques with her—reflexology, polarity balancing, aroma-therapy massage, and deep-trance meditation. She was (and is) one of the best teachers around, and she was patient and knowledgeable. Through her, I discovered that I had a natural talent for massage. I was invited to work a couple days a week at a wonderful eclectic spa in Toronto called Mo's in a cool, funky part of town. Through word of mouth, I very quickly built a steadily flourishing clientele.

As soon as I began touching people, I started having strange and uncanny experiences. I picked up information about them, especially when I closed my eyes. I could "see" what appeared to be blotches of darker energy outlining their bodies, which showed me the places where they had the most tension. Sometimes I'd pick up on something that was particularly shadowy and dense, and I'd ask them if they had an old injury there. Nine times out of ten, the clients would say yes. We were all astounded by this, and my clients would ask, "Wow, how did you do that?" I'd reply, "I really don't know, but when I close my eyes and place my hand on your body, I can actually see it as if I'm looking at an x-ray. And then something just tells me where the pain is and where it comes from."

In the beginning, my hands hurt so much by the end of the day that I'd have to pack them in ice. Sometimes I'd wake up in the middle of the night, and they'd be pulsing with a strange energy; other nights they hurt so much that I cried myself to sleep. Then one day the pain just went away, but my ability remained. During this time, Yvonne was a great source of comfort to me. I felt that she understood me, since to her this phenomenon wasn't abnormal.

The Beginning of Service: Accepting the Gift

My decision to attend some small psychic-development classes would prove to be another life-altering choice. I felt like the little Dutch boy with his finger in the dam: As soon as I began the exercises and the studies that were suggested, the waters broke through the barriers, and I began swimming in the sea of my intuition. It was the richest, most fulfilling time I'd ever had in terms of the number of extraordinary experiences that began to take place both in and around me.

When I touched the people who came in for an aroma-therapy massage, I heard names and saw images in my mind that revealed events that had happened in their lives, things that they were concerned about, and opportunities that were approaching. Of course, to confirm what I thought I detected, I described all this to my clients—to my astonishment, I realized that I was indeed picking up very private things. Soon afterward, people began to book appointments just to talk to me, and thus my career as an intuitive counselor was born.

At the time, I struggled with the idea that beyond witnessing what was in the present or past of my clients, I appeared to be seeing into their future. Because I was committed to living my life one day at a time, I was compelled to question how I could reconcile two very different philosophies: If I believed on the one hand that it's crucial to live in the now, then what was I doing speaking to people about the future? In fact, my state of mind became further complicated by the fact that the experience of looking into the future didn't seem like I was observing from far away; rather, it always felt as if I were recalling something that had already happened. To this day, it's always as though I'm "remembering" what's to come, because the future feels exactly the same as the past or present to me.

During this formative time, I read about the idea of parallel universes in a book that presented quantum physics in lay terms. I believed that I might be remembering a story that had already happened from another world, because time didn't exist in the same place as it does now. Sometimes I saw more than one thing—more than one outcome—and I began to understand the nature of choice, cause, and effect. I saw the future as a place of potential and probability that we can influence—that we aren't passing preordained, absolutely determined destinies.

Birth in the Garden of Potential

The psychological and spiritual healing that I'd accomplished was starting to pay off in unexpected ways. I'd embarked on an intense journey of recovery: I began therapy around the sexual-abuse issues, studied *A Course in Miracles,* and attended a Unity Church. I also learned about the philosophy of Catherine Ponder, Florence Scovel Shinn, Mary Baker Eddy, and Dion Fortune; and gobbled up books on Science of Mind as fast as I could read them.

I went to a weekly meditation group run by a Tibetan lama, and I prayed and gave thanks each day. I developed conscious contact with a Higher Power—asking for guidance to do good works, praying and meditating, and conducting an in-depth self-appraisal—and I made amends to all the people I'd harmed. In the course of those two years, I freed myself from so much heavy baggage that the chatter in my head subsided considerably.

I now believe that at this time I was "pregnant" with my authentic self. I was living one day at a time, with as much humility as I could muster (although I was aware that my ego and its various wounds and poor programming would always be a part of my human experience). I'd faithfully followed the suggestions to open up my channels, and by doing all that intuitive development in conjunction with my inner-healing work, I gave birth to a healthier self—one who was capable of experiencing a rich, multisensory life in service to others. It made every single thing I'd ever gone through worthwhile.

With the return of my intuitive abilities, my life also took an unexpected turn. My daily prayer to be shown the truth about my life and how to live it was being answered. Even so, I was very reluctant to accept this as my profession, since—God forbid—people might see me as the stereo-typical gypsy psychic with big dangling earrings and a turban on my head, gazing into a crystal ball.

Inside, I still wanted to be the lead singer in a rock band. For six years, when I did readings I'd tell people, "I don't really do this. I'm actually a singer, so I probably won't be here next year . . . but thanks for coming." Yet in time, things began to change. Although I was still pursuing music, it was the intuitive readings that directed my life. I never solicited a client or advertised my services; my clients came to me strictly by word of mouth.

It was then 1991, and tragedy struck again: My father died of a stroke on my sister's birthday—she found him dead in his chair. In addition, my mother began to have horrible headaches, which were caused by the malignant brain tumor that would kill her just two years later. I was emotionally battered by all the losses and the fear of more. My band had also broken up at the same time that a long-term relation-ship ended. It turns out that I'd changed so much I no longer had anything in common with most of the individuals in my life who still connected me to my past.

I left a lot of people behind when I embarked on my new life because I wasn't the party girl anymore. Some of this was painful, as I had to reluctantly turn away from a few individuals. I chose a road less traveled . . . nonetheless, I forged ahead, following the glimmer of light toward what I now saw as my true calling (although I was still scared to accept it).

The only consistent experience during this time was my intuitive work. I was doing readings and holding my own version of Yvonne's intuitive-development seminar, with amazing results for both myself and others. I discovered that the more work I did on myself—continuing the process of digging deep into my psyche to clean out the old wounds and clear the weeds from my daily mental and spiritual garden—the more clarity I had, not just in my readings for others, but in my own life as well.

I found that I was no longer just observing the universe on behalf of others, but was able to sense it for myself. I began to know how to navigate the world intuitively with less intellectual resistance, and I started to see through the eyes of my spirit. The door to wholeness had never been locked—I'd only believed that it was. As I began to listen to my inner voice, I started to witness miracles unfolding. My own spiritual growth became the bedrock of the service that I was able to provide for others.

≫≪ ≫≪ ≫≪

Chapter 6

STRANGE,
UNDENIABLE HAPPENINGS

One sunny, hot afternoon in June of 1992, I went for a walk. It wasn't a particularly special day, nor was it one when my meditation and prayer practice gave me any unusual hints or omens of what was to come. I decided to go to the local health-food store for my favorite coconut macaroons, and thinking of nothing remotely spiritual (although by some accounts savoring those cookies could be considered Divine!), I crossed the street. The moment that I stepped onto the opposite curb, my awareness abruptly shifted.

As I looked around, I felt that I was seeing with my eyes as if the body that I inhabited was simply a suit that had holes in it for me to peer through. It was completely jarring because I couldn't tell how tall I was in relation to the pavement. People walked by me on the street, not speaking . . . yet I could hear their thoughts chattering away like a cacophonous sea of noise.

I started to understand that something unusual was happening to my perception, and I allowed myself to relax. All the noises began to blend into a drone that resounded in one long, harmonic note that I knew held every sound in the universe. It was incredible—not just because it was beautiful, but because it felt as if every cell in my body recognized that note as the music of all life.

I was awestruck. I knew that I'd never be alone: I was a tiny part of this animate pulse that sounded through me as if I were a string on a celestial instrument played by the life force itself. I was humbled by its magnitude and by the absolute connection between every living thing.

Then, suddenly, there was no sound at all—everything became quiet. I thought that I'd gone deaf, but what I felt in the stillness around me was peace. After that, the sound began to slowly return until it was all that I could hear. Every deception in my mind was immediately revealed and deconstructed by the sound, revealing only the truth.

I was no longer afraid of anything, even my own death, because I knew with certainty that I was always present, even as dust. I realized that my individual life was meaning-ful. I wasn't frightened to look at myself anymore, and I was filled with the courage to change the things that I knew I was able to. As an all-encompassing feeling of compassion hit me like a wave, the keys to life were all there in the truth of the moment, and I was overcome with reverence. Eventually I started to feel more grounded in myself, and I found myself back on the sidewalk, staring down at the ground.

As soon as the sound filled me, I noticed a little blade of grass growing through the pavement. I understood in the deepest part of my being that we are all part of this uni-versal life force: that even the grass was made of the same stuff that I was, and within it was the intelligence of God. I started to cry as the enormity of this realization overcame me . . . I felt so insignificant. But as I stared at that single piece of grass courageously reaching up from the concrete, I recognized that it was a part of me. For one wonderful moment, I acknowledged life—the vastness of it all, and the "beingness" that's so crucial to living in the moment. I felt the presence of a Higher Power, and I knew a love in my heart unlike what I'd experienced at any other time in my life.

I believe that life is love—not the kind that you read about in romance novels, but love in its true creative form. It allows the Divine to take shape in an expression of life that's an ever-sustaining circle. We're given life by this love that lives through us to create more life. Each of us is blessed with the ability to choose how and what we create. I've never forgotten, nor will I ever fail to recall, the impact of that event in my search for spiritual meaning in my life.

The Result—Understanding Faith and Intuition

As more and more people came to me for readings, I began to observe and understand a common dilemma we all seem to share. One of the biggest issues facing us is the drive not just for material and emotional security, but also for spiritual sustenance and a sense of belonging. So many of us are motivated by fear and lack, yet at a deeper level we *know* that there's more to life. I realize now that this connection to the greater world of the soul is available to us all, and the greatest hurdle is our ego, which keeps us locked into a limited, five-sensory, mechanistic perception of the universe.

Given my religious upbringing, I always saw God as being "out there"—somewhere above me personally. I felt that I had to beseech heaven to intervene on my behalf in my life or that I needed to talk to a priest or minister in order to reach God. I didn't realize that my soul was a *part* of the awareness of the Divine and if I listened to it, I could act and experience the world guided by a higher knowing *within* me.

I remember the first time I heard the references to the indwelling Christ Consciousness, the Buddha Mind, the Higher Self, and the prayer "Thy will be done through me." I realized that my faith had to include an alignment with a higher set of spiritual principles than my ego desires. If I made that connection each day, I could and would receive higher guidance. Simply put, I had to trust that there was something greater than myself that could transform me into a better person—that I could find meaning in my own existence and in being of service to the world around me.

I began experiencing a remarkable clarity with respect to my gift. I developed faith and understood how in committing to a soul-based life, I'd be led by my intuition to engage more fully in the world. And that's exactly what happened. My first real experience with faith came during those early days when all kinds of synchronicities and miracles began to unfold, showing me that my life hadn't been wasted. It was also through faith that I realized that through conscious alignment and intention, I could not only heal myself, but could also be connected to the Divine and—by extension—help others heal through my example.

It was this organic, action-based relationship between a higher spiritual intelligence and myself that helped me open up to the inner teacher-guardian that I call "intuition." My faith was all about trusting that there was a

Higher Power, a source that I could tap in to through prayer. When I acted as if I trusted that it would lead me to something, it invariably did. As my intuitive abilities began to show up more frequently and consistently, I had to have faith that my sixth sense was real and not just a figment of my imagination.

When I began to act on this blind trust and shared what I saw with others, I received consistent confirmation that I was on the right track and something profound was happening to me. (As an aside, I've never received anything but signs of truth when I've asked for them. I don't always know the form they'll take, but that part is unimportant—the *action* of faith is the key. We need to trust in the higher will of Divine order and allow it to reveal its nature according to its own timetable.)

Inspired by my experiences and the support from my ongoing metaphysical studies, I launched a seminar called "The Soul, The Ego, and The Artist" to help people recover access to their intuition by examining the roles of the soul, the ego, and personal responsibility in creating reality. The seminar was a great success, and I was invited to a number of cities to present my version of this universal concept. Even the most skeptical attendees were shocked by what they found they were capable of by the end of the day. I continued to feel encouraged as proof of what I'd experienced in my own life began to show up for others.

Giant Angels Toss a Baby

My childhood nanny, Mrs. Kelly, had told me that when I saw an angel, I had to have faith that it was real, because I could trust its presence. That was fine when I was a kid, but as I've matured, the innocence of that statement has taken on a new meaning. I've always considered myself a bit of a skeptic . . . I have to see it to believe it. I've also been reluctant to claim any total explanation of my experiences, because I know that I don't have all the facts—just the evidence of experience, which for me is absolute and true. But I know that angels are real because I've seen and experienced one.

One day I met with Yvonne to demonstrate a new massage technique I'd developed that was accompanied by spoken-word visualization—that is, meditation. It was a really effective method of relaxation, and it was clearly having a positive impact on my clients. I began Yvonne's massage the same way as always, standing behind her and moving my hands rhythmically up her spine and around the shoulders as I spoke my initial prayer for guidance, protection, and healing. I followed this with spoken meditation, saying, "On a white sandy beach by an enchanted ocean in a place called Sanctuary," and what occurred after about ten minutes was astounding.

I experienced my spirit being lifted up out of my body as if it were merely the container of my consciousness. It felt as though a force that was part of me but not under my direction was pulling me out. I heard my voice continue to speak the words of the meditation, and I felt the rhythm of my arms moving at a distance until the five-sensory experience dissolved altogether. I found myself in a strange new environment, fully aware and conscious—and very surprised. I was surrounded by grainy light, which I've come to recognize as a signal that I've entered the peripheral dimension that I sometimes find myself in during readings or deep meditative states. I was, however, keenly aware of being transferred from one realm to the other—from my ordinary reality to this other place, which had very obvious characteristics that were both like and unlike my usual day-to-day experience.

I found myself in front of a huge door that I couldn't see the top of, and I noticed that the bottom had enough space for me to crawl under. As I did so, I entered a huge courtyard with stone archways towering into cloudy air and bright beams of light shining down onto the floor, which looked like a black-and-white chessboard. Something more solid appeared in front of me; and I saw a huge, 30-foot tall creature with what appeared to be wings looming over me. It had no face—just a blinding, bright light that observed me with total comprehension.

At first I was really frightened, because I'd never felt so exposed and "known" by anything in my life. I truly thought that this being could see everything about me that I couldn't, and the feeling was terribly unnerving. I remember wondering aloud if this was what an angel was. It picked me up, and I found myself cradled among its weblike feathers. They seemed to be made of light, white threads—part web, part feather, part something else—that sparkled with teeny flecks of color.

My mind raced as I touched the being. I began to get excited because I realized that this was a real angel. Then it dawned on me that other people must have seen such creatures before, and that's why they're depicted with feathered wings. A deep, resonant humming sound came from within the angel, enveloping me in absolute peace, acceptance, and love as I relaxed into a complete state of awe and wonder at what was happening.

The angel walked with me down a corridor of huge trees (which were unlike earthly ones) into an open place where there were ten more beings. I was completely unnerved as the one that was carrying me tossed me into the air, and they all began to hum and then laugh. At least it sounded like laughter—it was a joyful sound and strangely playful, and these 11 angels tossed me around as if I were a ball.

Then, completely unexpectedly, I fell into a bright purple, cloudy fabric that dissolved beneath me, breaking my fall into a pool of water. I looked around, but the angels were gone. I was in another place, and I felt as if I were being baptized at the base of a crystal mountain where everything sparkled and hummed a heavenly sound. Before I could get my bearings, I felt myself being sucked downward into my body and back into the room—where I was still doing the massage. I put my feet on as if they were shoes.

I was completely present but breathing more deeply than usual. At this point I stopped the massage, and Yvonne turned her head and looked at me—her deep blue eyes almost glowed for a minute, and her pupils were fully dilated. I told her, "You'll never believe what just happened!"

She replied, "Colette, I had the most extraordinary vision that I need to share with you." She then proceeded to tell me that when we began the massage, she went into a deep meditation, where she had a vision that I crawled beneath a huge door. She followed me under it and saw not me, but the back of a huge angelic creature. She followed it into a long corridor that opened up into a courtyard where there were many more angels standing in a circle. She said that the one she'd followed had a newborn in its arms, and they all took turns holding the baby and tossing it in the air as it gurgled and laughed. She found herself wondering where she was, but the beings disappeared in a cloud of dazzling violet and white smoke. She turned her head and found herself back on the table looking up at me.

I was flabbergasted, but this was enough for me to realize that it wasn't just a dream that I'd conjured up or fabricated. I trusted with every fiber of my being that what I'd experienced was real, and I knew that I would be altered in some way. From that day forward, my readings began to have a different, enhanced sense of spirituality to them, and more people started to find out about me through word of mouth. Even now, whenever I'm in doubt, I remember my angel. And when I recall that experience, I'm reminded that I have the power to help people, and I'm not alone.

≫ ≪

No matter how hard I tried to cajole the universe into connecting me to my angel, I had no further visitations for a couple of years. Then something happened: For three consecutive nights, I saw a face looking at me as I fell asleep: Once I saw a benevolent and smiling Jesus; another time I saw an Indian sage with dark skin and flowing white robes; and a third time I clearly saw Mary Magdalene, who spoke to me, saying, "I am the Magdalene, named Mary. Remember the goddess"—and then disappeared.

A week later, while I was making myself comfortable before my morning meditation, my little dog, Gizmo, marched over to me and stared into my eyes. He sat down on my lap just as I was about to start, and I decided to let him stay there, closing my eyes.

I don't know how long it took, but as soon as I settled into my meditation, I was transported back to the grainy, light-filled place that I knew as the peripheral dimension. I was sitting at the edge of the same crystal mountain I'd seen when I met my angel. I could feel an amazing sense of calm protection as the wing of my angel enveloped me.

I asked it, "Where have you been? Why haven't you come before now?" And in a wordless hum I heard, *Have faith and trust in me—I am always here.* Then it all disappeared.

Since that day, I've never doubted the existence of angels, the connection we have to them, or any of my experiences with them. Although I still consider myself a devout skeptic, I have an unerring faith in God, goodness, and the Divine intelligence that's around and within us. No matter how and what I need to learn in this lifetime, I trust that I'll always be where I need to be. We must believe that when our intuition tells us to go left instead of right, it may be because an angel is waiting around the corner.

≫≪ ≫≪ ≫≪

Chapter 7

FULL-TIME INTUITIVE

So many people began booking readings—as one friend told another, who told another—that I no longer had time for my aromatherapy practice. I did readings full-time and threw myself with gusto into pursuing my musical career.

It was 1993, and my mother died that February. Although there was an undeniably fierce love between the two of us, we had a tumultuous relationship. I remember how quickly she deteriorated after her cancer was diagnosed and how powerless I felt. Yet this was also the first time in my life that I predicted a death (other than the baker's when I was little).

I'd come back from visiting Mom in the hospital, and she seemed to be in good spirits. Nevertheless, when I got home, I decided to play with my tarot cards, dropping a few on the floor. I turned up Death, the Ace of Swords, and a Queen—the three-card formation that I'd learned I never wanted to see, and I knew it was a clear portent that my mother was going to die. An hour later, the hospital called to tell me that my mother had indeed slipped into a coma. I went back to say my good-byes, and she passed on to the "other side" that night. Even though I knew that she was going to a better place, I was devastated by her death and the remorse for what I couldn't change between us.

Prayers for Music

I had a music manager at that time who'd put me in touch with a talented producer in New York, so I spent some time there pursuing my dream. The loss of my parents gave me a lot of emotional creativity—I needed an outlet to express it, which the music gave me. I took a month off from readings to concentrate on it exclusively.

Although I was really proud of my songs and what I'd accomplished, and I received a lot of positive and encouraging feedback from the music industry, I was nonetheless led to a number of disappointing experiences. Many individuals expressed interest in my record and told me how great it was, but no matter how many deals were offered, something would thwart them: One time the company suddenly went out of business; on another occasion, the person who loved what I was doing moved across the country. Although lots of people said that I was talented and they wanted to offer me an opportunity, nothing ever came of it. Every door that opened was quickly slammed shut. I was devastated.

Now at that point I was well versed in metaphysics, having studied the subject in depth. Every time I'd experience something new that I didn't understand, I found a book, took a course, or otherwise did something to grasp the mechanics of it. I knew that the world I saw was a direct result of my thinking and inner beliefs. Each day I read for five or six people, and their experiences proved to me that this concept held true for others as well.

I was also aware that holding a belief as a given and picturing a desire as already having happened in the now would activate the "Law of Attraction"—if I practiced this technique, I'd inevitably create the opportunities that I wanted. I knew without a doubt that a combination of creative visualization, affirmation, tithing (the practice of giving away 10 percent of one's income to a church or charity), and prayer was the most powerful method of creating an abundant reality. Yet I did everything right and failed . . . so what was going on?

I'd been an avid student of Catherine Ponder, and I took a statement in her book *The Dynamic Laws of Prayer* as absolute truth: "When you pray, you stir into action an atomic force. You release a potent spiritual vibration that can be released in no other way. Through prayer you unleash a God energy within and around you that gets busy working for you and through you, producing right attitudes, reactions, and results." I was holding seminars based on my version of this concept, and it was working for people. So why wasn't it doing the same for me? I thought, *Is God giving me a second chance at life with all this talent, only to slam the door in my face?*

Each day I prayed that I would be used as an instrument for positive change; and I willed that the universe, my guides, and the angels would help me realize my dream of being a singer/songwriter. I prayed that it would be effortless to see how to do the right thing for the highest good of all concerned. I asked that opportunities be presented so that I could do beneficial work with my God-given talents.

To make sure that I was being clear, I'd add: *My God-given talents . . . you know, singing. In case You didn't hear me,*

God, I really, really, really see myself getting a record deal and quitting the readings. It's been fun; I learned a lot, but time to move on, right? Bigger fish to fry and all that. Oh, yeah—Thy will be done. Amen.

I prayed, did affirmations, listened to my intuition, and watched closely for signs and omens.

The readings kept coming.

The music failed.

I prayed some more, asking for the angels to clear my intuitive channels, since I thought they might be clogged.

More readings and more people wanting seminars came my way.

The music failed.

I prayed harder.

Did I mention that my music career continued to tank?

I prayed and prayed; spoke and wrote affirmations; tithed on top of tithing; used creative visualization; and did silly, stupid angel dances. I asked for a billboard to appear that would tell me exactly where I needed to be in order to be of service. I thought, *Thy will be done. . . .*

And then the phone rang. "I want to make an appointment," said a heavily accented male voice.

"Where are you calling from?"

"India."

After a shocked silence on my end, I cleared my throat and acted nonchalant: "Don't you have enough people with my abilities over there?"

"Well, madam, I heard about you in an airport, and I felt compelled to call and tell you how valuable you are to the world. The people who spoke of you said many things confirming that I must contact you. I humbly ask to make an appointment."

I gave him an appointment . . . and surrendered.

I got the message, so I reluctantly let the music go and saw what I'd really prayed for. This has since become one of my favorite stories to tell in my intuitive-development seminars when I explain how to manifest reality through prayer.

I Don't Speak the Language,
but My Intuition Does!

My seminar "The Soul, The Ego, and The Artist" continued to grow in popularity, and I began to attract clients from all over Canada and the U.S. Then people started telling their friends in the U.K., Europe, South America, China, and Japan; and my client base expanded further.

At one point, a client who worked for a Japanese magazine booked an appointment for two lovely women visiting Toronto from Japan. I was very excited because I'd done readings for only a few people in that country, and they were mostly Americans or Canadians working abroad. These would be my first clients coming directly from Japan.

When the women arrived, they were so polite. They bowed, and I bowed, and then they bowed again. I wasn't sure what to do next. Their host had left them with me but had forgotten to tell me a very important piece of information: Neither spoke a word of English. I was completely discombobulated.

There they were, smiling, each holding a cassette tape for her session; and there I was, sweating, wondering how I was going to do it. My style of giving readings was to rapidly interpret images that I saw in my mind's eye, telling the clients what I observed and asking if it made sense to them. If it did and they confirmed the validity of what I saw, this gave my intuitive senses permission to move on to the next image. If they didn't know, I'd revisit the image until we knew how it applied to their past or present. Although no one was allowed to say anything but yes or no, our exchange *was* important. . . . Now how was this going to work?

I thought, *When in doubt, ask an angel.*

I asked one of them to wait in the living room while I took the other with me into the kitchen for the reading. After figuring out where everybody was supposed to go, I sat with the first woman and prayed. I asked whatever angel was close to me to make friends with the one by her side and translate for me—because I was in trouble.

Immediately, a fuzzy kind of pale light began to show up around me. I was suddenly very calm as I slipped into the peripheral location of awareness where I experience my intuition. Images were coming to me rapidly for the first few minutes, and I just talked to the tape recorder, explaining what I saw.

What was uncanny was that I had another mind split, much like when my abilities returned full force during my rape at 19. This time it reminded me of two computer screens, both visible at the same time. There was no violent jarring; rather, it was a gentle experience as I saw myself shift from one perception to another. I viewed the session from two perspectives: (1) I saw that if I remained attached to the form of the reading, I'd cut myself off from a lot of information; and (2) I was shown that I should release the expectation that dialogue between us was necessary as confirmation. I recognized that by letting go, I'd be able to view the whole "movie" and not just snippets. It took some courage, because I still favored what I knew and was familiar with, but I went for it.

After the women left, I felt pretty good but was still unsure, as this was a new experience for me. The next day, the women's host called to say that she'd translated the tapes for both of them, and although I'd had trouble with a couple of Japanese names, my new clients were ecstatic. Indeed, the information that I'd relayed about events in their past and present and the direction they were heading was very accurate.

So I learned a very interesting lesson: If I allow myself to be attached to the belief in a particular form, I might miss the greater spiritual message. By surrendering the form, I found out that my inner teacher-guardian is a master of all languages! The only limit to intuition is the mind that it's filtered through.

Filters—Clear or Clogged?

I began observing something that I consider key to my beliefs about how we hear our intuitive voice. I realized that when I applied my mental faculties toward finding the connection—for example, expecting that a rigid system of instructions would provide a result—I was filtering information through whatever state of mind I was in at the time. Almost everyone who shared their experiences with me (especially those who were putting a lot of effort into opening themselves up to their intuitive abilities) was doing the same thing.

The language we have at our disposal to individually and collectively explain our sixth sense is too limited. We all run spiritual phenomena through the filter of our personalities and life experiences because it feels like the safest thing to do. We're at varied levels of consciousness and are influenced by things that help us translate the unfamiliar intuitive language into something that we understand. For example, if we have a strong religious influence that suggests to us that psychic phenomena are evil, we'll be afraid and project that fear onto our experience.

But intuition doesn't operate within a dogmatic form or the system of beliefs that the rational mind has settled on. Rather, the intellect and all its learned habits need to be acknowledged as a handicap and surrendered. If we want to take full advantage of our natural birthright, we must unlearn many things about the way that we live our lives and project our thoughts.

This is no easy task—especially if a person has the gift that allows access to the place of the soul, but he or she still lives and breathes in a paradigm that's threatened by it. The only way to a steady and unobstructed connection to the intuitive voice is to make sure that the filter through which it's experienced is clear. (In Part II, I'll explain how to clear *your* filter.)

Sex and the Single Psychic

As much as I was enjoying my newfound popularity, I still had to deal with other people's attitudes and prejudices toward what I was doing. I met a man who came from a conservative Jewish background who was funny, sweet, opinionated, and well educated. He loved books as much as I did, and he laughed at the same ridiculous jokes that I liked. We enjoyed each other's company immensely. Although I didn't practice Judaism, I was considered datable because my mother was Jewish (even though I was raised as a Christian and favored the teachings of Jesus).

I was still toying with what to call myself. Psychic? Clairvoyant? I was at an ambivalent phase of my career and didn't feel comfortable labeling my profession. I think that when I met this man, his hormones must have obstructed his hearing because I do remember saying that I worked as a psychic when he got around to asking what I did. However, about three months later, he completely freaked out when I mentioned that I couldn't meet him for dinner because I was hosting "You Are Psychic" for The Learning Annex. He said that he could never bring me home to meet his parents because of his religion and its opinion of my profession. I cried. He left. He never called me again. There went my dream of shalom in the home!

Next was the cute firefighter who totally sparked my interest when he walked into the room. He really, really liked me—until he saw the tarot cards on my kitchen table. He said, "My mother 'sees' things and she's totally whacked . . . I gotta go."

Okay. Bye.

Next was a wine steward. Now we all know *that* was a mistake, considering that I'm a recovered alcoholic! But he was *so* good-looking, and he said that he meditated, as well knowing astrology and all kinds of other things. Hooray! He loved what I did for a living and told me that intuitive sight ran in *his* family. I figured that I could handle the wine part. But he'd ask, "Okay, what do you see about me now?" at the most inopportune moments. And when he introduced me to his friends, they all inquired about the same things: "What am I thinking?" "Hey, what lottery ticket should I buy?" and "Who's gonna win the game?"

Okay. Bye.

Then I met a wonderful, bright, handsome, terrific lawyer, and we got along like a house on fire. He was Irish

Catholic—a yummy guy who brought me flowers and a giant box of expensive Belgian chocolates, took me to dinner a few times, and then made my toes curl when he kissed me on the fourth date. He invited me to his home in the Bahamas for the weekend . . . so romantic. *Sigh.*

I thought that I'd better tell him what I did for a living, deciding on "clairvoyant counselor." We went to a beautiful fancy-schmancy restaurant. Never mind dessert—I fled once the conversation turned in the direction of saving my soul from the "Prince of Darkness." I cried my eyes out when I got home and ate the whole box of chocolates. Forget the bikini and the Bahamas.

After that, a well-meaning friend invited me to a swanky singles party brimming with available men. I agreed to go, but I wanted to know what she'd told them about me first, since I hated small talk and usually avoided discussing my profession. It turns out that she'd let it be known that I went to a chichi private school and spent time in Switzerland. She also let it slip to one curious person that I almost died from a drug overdose but was "now a recovered alcoholic/addict who conversed with a 30-foot angel, taught people how to see auras, and talked to dead people once in a while." I spent the entire interminable evening in misery, as I was plum out of cute and funny retorts.

Enter another lawyer—a very sharp and conversational criminal attorney. When we met I was sober, so I could articulate well, and I really liked him. Flirting commenced, and I just knew that the phone-number exchange was going to happen . . . but I was in intuitive denial. Two hours later he said, "You haven't told me what you do for a living."

So I did.

"I don't believe in that."

Okay. Bye.

Now I do understand that some people can be tremendously suspicious and fearful, thinking that we "intuitively abled" types have some kind of potentially intrusive power; or else through lack of education, they see psychics/intuitives as stereotypical charlatans. But I was unprepared for the personal rejections. I wasn't living among the committed New Age community where everyone believed as I did. I was the person everyone told their amazing stories of the supernatural to, and I was getting shunned because of it—mostly by men, I might add. It was a difficult time, especially since I really wanted to get married.

One might wonder why I couldn't have predicted all this. Well, one of the biggest blocks in the part of your mind that filters intuition is desire, because it hides those red flags. Have you ever wanted an outcome so badly you could taste it? . . . Bye-bye, intuition; hello, desire! It was a lesson that took a long time to learn, and even though I could easily spot the issue in my clients, my personal "boyfriend radar" was completely off the intuitive mark, and my "inner traffic lights" were backward. Although I didn't see it at the time, the world—and especially the men I was attracting—mirrored in Technicolor my own conflicted ambivalence.

If My Husband Answers, Say That You're My Hairdresser

It wasn't just the men I was meeting who were behaving as if I did something strange and therefore suspect. For a while, it seemed as if I were the biggest secret around. I was still having trouble getting used to people calling for appointments and leaving strange instructions on my machine. Here are some examples of what I heard:

- "If I don't answer, please don't leave a message. I don't want my family to know I'm coming to see you."

- "My husband can't know I'm coming, so . . . um . . . I'll just have to call back."

- "My wife will think I'm nuts, so you have to promise not to say that I was there."

- "Hi, this is Marilyn. I'd like to make an appointment to come as soon as possible. Here's my number, but if my husband answers, please, please say that you're my new hairdresser—I'd so appreciate it. Thanks. I'm sure you understand."

Well, I did and I didn't. This attitude was very disturbing because I was struggling with a deep need for approval. However, I was quickly learning that this would have to be eradicated from my wish list if I was going to be okay with myself and hold my head up with any integrity at all. There was a lot of fear that I had to face, both within me and on behalf of the people who sought my counsel—guidance that came to them through the very technique they seemed to be fighting against.

What became so obvious to me was that not only was *I* a secret, but I'd also turned into the person who held everybody else's. I was the one at the party someone would inevitably corner, saying, "Please, may I have a word with you? I have no one else to talk to about this—I have prescient dreams, and my husband thinks I'm crazy, but I know I'm not."

It was not atypical on a Tuesday afternoon for me to be talking to a man on the International Olympic Committee about visions he'd experienced and couldn't decipher, or chatting with a celebrity (who will, of course, remain nameless) who just had to understand why she couldn't meet her dead father in her dreams anymore. It also wouldn't be unusual for me to encounter a housewife who knew about world events months in advance but was terrified because she was a born-again Christian, and there were rules against that sort of thing—never mind coming to see me!

It was a time of great learning for me as I allowed my gift to lead my life. I met doctors who arrived curious but left convinced. I encountered people with various levels of education and all manner of religious backgrounds who were looking for one thing: someone to let them know that their own experiences were real, that they were understood and not alone. I found that I was able to tap in to a connection with the person in front of me that convinced us both that somehow there's more to life.

We know when we've individually and collectively tuned in to this mystery. I still believe that calling all of it "the mystery" is the most honest descriptor, since language is so incredibly limiting when we insist on labeling what can't be fully expressed with words. It occurred to me that my role as a reader was to be my clients' witness. I began to think that doing intuitive readings was like narrating someone's story: As I revealed the personal history and potential future of the individual in front of me, it was much like reading a book and then recounting it to him or her.

Thinking of myself as a witness or storyteller made it easier to bear when I was frequently told, "We have to keep these conversations to ourselves—after all, what would 'they' think?" I decided to make it my mission to help bring this fear and confusion to a place where everyone would understand. Then I started having weird dreams about being burned at the stake, so I filed away that well-intentioned idea, realizing I'd have to wait until *I* didn't care what "they" thought of me.

The Third Eye Winks!

During this period, I began to have a recurring experience when I closed my eyes to meditate or fall asleep: a vision of a big, beautiful, wide-open golden eye blinking at me. I'd open my eyes and there would be nothing unusual—no lights in the room or anything abnormal. Then I'd close them, and it would appear again. Its center would be bright blue, violet, or green, but its shape and essence were identical every time.

I was loosely studying kundalini yoga at a center down the street, and the yogini told me that it was a sign that my third eye was opening to the world. It was reminding me that my psychic sight was truly present and available to me.

It was weird for a while, as though I were being watched from inside myself. I was very aware of doing things that weren't particularly enlightened, such as gossiping or being competitive, judgmental, intolerant, or self-righteous. It was as if I had an inner watcher to patrol my mind. The eye itself wasn't judgmental, just observant. So one day I decided to talk to it, and out loud I said: "Okay, eye, if you're really watching me, you must have a purpose beyond that, and I'd like to know what it is. Show me a sign that you've heard me!"

I closed my eyes, but it wasn't there, nor did it come back for a few days. Then I was at the dentist's, and when

I closed my eyes, there it was spontaneously, and this time it winked at me . . . at least it had a sense of humor! What was really fun was that lots of my students were having the same experience when they practiced the meditations that I gave them. Third eyes were winking and blinking all over town in those days!

※※ ※※ ※※

Chapter 8

A SWAMI IN SUBURBIA

My friend Beth and I were sharing a lovely walk-up apartment in an old Victorian house in downtown Toronto. Both of us were tired of the single life and wanted to connect with that "special someone."

Beth had a business in India that was flourishing, and she traveled back and forth a lot, leaving me for long stretches to contemplate my single life. I was aware that another path was calling me, but I didn't know where it was. In time Beth fell in love—she sold her business and was going to stay in Canada, settle down with her man, buy a house in the country, and have a baby. I was happy for her, but I really wanted to find a guy and get married, too.

I knew that certain metaphysical tools could help activate the Law of Attraction, so I decided to go for the gusto and create a dream board to help draw my beloved to me. When I first learned about this intuitive tool, I was told that it was a means of letting the universe know what I wanted, yet I'd never made one before with this goal in mind. In a dream board, your aspiration is symbolized in both a picture and a written affirmation, and the idea is that by meditating on the goal each day and visualizing it as if it were a reality in your current life, you'll help attract and create the events and circumstances that will support it. Then the board is released after a set period of time, usually a year after it's created. In the interim, you maintain an awareness of any signs, omens, or intuitive messages that may lead you toward your goal.

I didn't know if this tool would be successful in attracting a husband, but I was willing to try. I'd done general dream boards in the past that had all worked—although often not in the manner that I'd expected or within the time frame I'd hoped for. Nonetheless, they invariably did what I set out for them to do. For example, I found a beautiful photo of a lovely desert scene featuring a Joshua tree (which I'd never seen before). I put it on a board with an affirmation accompanying it that stated: "This year, I travel to new and exciting places." Eight months later, I visited the desert in California to do a photo shoot in a place I'd never been to—by no coincidence it was called Joshua Tree.

You might be wondering what a dream board looks like exactly. Well, they're very easy to make: Simply draw a border around the perimeter of a large piece of artist-quality bristol board to signal to the universe your intention to manifest the images and affirmations found within it. Place a spiritual symbol centered at the top in order to signify pure intent—for example, you may choose a depiction of an angel, a cross, a picture of Jesus, or a Buddhist symbol. Then, in the very middle of the board, place a tiny photo of yourself in which you're smiling and happy. Use images that you've cut out of magazines, drawn, or photographed that evoke the *feeling* of what you intend to create and magnetize by the Law of Attraction. For example, you might choose depictions of fresh fruits and vegetables for good health, or images of people laughing together for rewarding friendships . . . anything that gives a sense of the essence of what's desired. At the bottom of the board, I always include a statement such as "This, or something better, now manifests for me and for the highest good of all concerned."

So I thought I'd try this technique to find a husband. I created my dream board, filling it with pictures of happy couples smiling and kissing, a beautiful bride, and photographs of men who all looked alike: tall, dark, and handsome. I met Steve just a few months later. My profession didn't intimidate him—in fact, he thought it was cool. That (and the fact that he looked exactly like the men on my dream board) was enough for me. We quickly fell into hormonal bliss, which we took to be love. Just as I'd wanted, he asked me to marry him . . . and of course I said yes!

But the first night I met him something had happened that I'd ignored. As he held my hand, I heard my inner voice clearly say, *This is not your husband!* Details, details. . . . It kept bothering me, and I remembered it as I agreed to his proposal. But I wanted to be married, so I moved to the outskirts of town to be with this young, handsome, decent, great guy. My friends started teasing me by calling me the "swami in the suburbs."

Although I experienced a nagging discomfort on a deep, intuitive level, I felt that I was supposed to marry him anyway—that it was "right" to do so when I did. It put us both on an extraordinary yet painful journey of self-understanding that revealed the areas where we both needed to heal if we were ever to achieve a healthy relationship. I grew so much in the rich, mucky fertilizer he and I created together, facing myself with as much fearless honesty as I could. Still, it was very painful. The marriage didn't last, but I'll never say that it was a mistake (nor would he), as we had so much to learn from each other, equally sharing the burden of our unresolved wounds and our subsequent transformation.

Our lesson was that we get what we want, but it's not always what it appears to be. I knew that our marriage wouldn't last; however, my intuition pushed me to experience it because I needed to look at all the things within me that actually prevented me from participating in a healthy, respectful, nurturing, and loving relationship.

Sometimes we're led directly into the darkness by our intuition because we must face certain issues in order to finally heal and find joy. On these occasions, we have to trust that it's a necessary—albeit painful—process that will allow us to be released from the bondage of those things that keep us from really *knowing* ourselves and our place in the world. When we think that we're moving backward, if we're willing to peel back the layers and face the truth about who we are, we can put ourselves on a spiritual path that takes us forward.

So in the end, a lot of good came out of our marriage. For example, Steve encouraged me to step out of my fear of becoming known on a larger scale for my work. Before we got married, I'd turned down a lot of media opportunities, clinging to the idea that I must never solicit clients—that if I were the "real deal," people would find me through word of mouth. I was ambivalent about using my gift, so I eschewed advertising of any kind and held the misguided belief that bringing attention to this part of my life might result in the loss of my ability. I struggled with who I was, and I hoped that marriage would help me find a new identity—but of course, it actually showed me that the role of suburban housewife wasn't for me! With Steve's encouragement, I accepted a prestigious opportunity to write the first New Age monthly column in Canada's fashion magazine *Flare,* and I began to take my work more seriously.

Hand of Fate

I met Alex, who was from Santa Fe, New Mexico, when she was visiting Toronto. She and I had a strange and uncanny instant connection—I was *sure* that I knew her already, although I didn't. I also felt that we were going to work together on something but brushed the feeling aside. When I have a really clear connection with a client, it's as if I'm watching TV, and it was like that with Alex: When I began to look at her energy, I was overloaded with images, as if I were switching channels with a remote.

She sat down, and I began to describe a young woman on a horse and other images that seemed somehow related but weren't. She stopped me to explain that I was describing all the photographs of relatives that she'd been compiling that morning. I went on to describe in detail a film project that she was working on with her husband, telling her how it would look and that it would take them on a trip around the globe. She confirmed this, adding that it was about exploring the lives of people with particular intuitive, psychic, and spiritual gifts. She asked me if I might be interested in participating, but I declined her offer.

A year later my friend and former roommate, Beth, who'd spent some time in Santa Fe, needed a few of her belongings that she'd left there. I remembered that that's where Alex lived, and I began to search for her number. A few hours later, the phone rang: It was Alex, who asked me if I'd take a look at her proposal and recommend someone else for her film since I'd said that I wasn't interested. Clearly something very important was about to happen—I felt electricity run down my arms as I told her that I'd just been looking for her number. I was very aware that the synchronicity was meaningful and larger than the coincidence that had connected us that day.

The next day, a FedEx envelope from Alex (containing her proposal) arrived at the door while I was talking to Steve about an unrelated TV opportunity that I'd turned down. I remember his words as clearly as if they were spoken yesterday. He said, "You know, Colette, you were given this extraordinary gift that obviously helps people. What do you think you're accomplishing by withholding it from others? What right do you have to hide it when it was obviously given freely to you?" I didn't even open the FedEx package. Instead, I called Alex in Santa Fe and agreed to do her film. It was called *Hand of Fate*—a documentary featuring six intuitively gifted individuals, and it included interviews and footage of the Nechung State Oracle of His Holiness the Dalai Lama in Dharamsala, accompanied by a musical score by Eric Rosse and Tori Amos.

Although I was initially afraid, I spoke openly about my gift, what it was like living with it, and how it felt to have pushed my music aside for it. The documentary was shown across the world in many film festivals, broadening my international client base as viewers connected to my story and found ways to contact me. I met some of the most important people in my life because of that film. Agreeing to participate made me accountable for sharing my gift with others, regardless of my fears.

Spinning Wheels and Cosmic Cookies

Shortly after I met Alex, I put together a recording of my most popular spoken-word meditations, based on the chakra system that I used in all my seminars. The chakras are an Eastern philosophical model of the mind-body-spirit interface that's said to exist in the energy body of all human beings. The word *chakra* comes from the Sanskrit, meaning "wheel," and it serves to describe a spinning wheel of bio-energy.

The seven main wheels correspond to the colors of the rainbow and span the base of the spine to the top of the head. The first wheel (at the base) is red and relates to issues of basic survival. The second is orange, ruling the emotions, creativity, and sexuality. The third is yellow and is associated with the ego and personal power/individuation. The fourth is green and rules social connection, love, and healing. The fifth is blue, representing communication. The sixth—the third eye—is violet and corresponds to intuition. The seventh and final chakra, found at the crown of the head, is white and represents divinity and all things spiritual.

The chakras are also believed to resonate to the seven musical notes of the C scale. It's been proven that visualization techniques accompanied by music and meditation can be extremely effective in healing, reenergizing, and clearing any blocks that may prevent a person from receiving intuitive information. To my knowledge, my recording was the first project that combined the elements of music, imagery, and guided spoken word for a mainstream audience.

My students originally all received the meditation, which was made on tape using prerecorded music. I had so many requests for the cassettes that I decided I had to record a much higher-quality version. With my background in music, I had a vision to create an ambitious meditation project where the score added impact to the experience, so I decided to partner with platinum-selling New Age artist Mars Lasar to create *Journey Through the Chakras*. After speaking with Mars (and with the gift of an airline ticket from my friends Tricia and Lance Secretan), I was on the plane to Los Angeles within 24 hours. We recorded the first three chakras as a demo, which I was going to present to record labels to see if I could garner any interest. It was an exciting process, as it was a marriage of both my musical and intuitive talents.

Another fortuitous and Divinely led connection was presented to me when I returned. I got a phone call from a friend in New York who said she had a strong hunch that I was about to meet a woman who lived in Toronto, and the minute I set eyes on Deenah, I knew that we were meant to do something important together. We had an immediate connection, becoming fast friends as we shared our mutual desire to help others by taking spirituality out of the closet and bringing it into everyday life. A trip to Martha's Vineyard together launched The Cosmic Cookie Company "for hungry minds and spirits," with *Journey Through the Chakras* as our first project. Shortly thereafter, I went back to L.A., and Mars and I completed the CD.

Within the first month of its release in Canada, it became the number one seller in major retail outlets across the country, with buyers calling us to reorder, curious about its rapid success. Deenah and I were thrilled, as our dream of bringing this meditation concept mainstream was obviously working. (It's since become a classic and is available through Hay House.)

It was obvious to me that my life was pointing in an undeniable direction. It was also around this time that Steve and I decided to separate. We'd gone to therapy together, which helped immensely when we split up. In fact, we went away on one last wonderful vacation together and parted as friends, honoring our journey and its gifts to each of us.

≫≪ ≫≪ ≫≪

Chapter 9

INTUITIVE DREAMS
BECOME REALITY

One of my clients was an executive in the recording industry, and I had a strong intuitive impression that our connection would extend beyond his session with me. I remember his first reading when he came to my home north of Toronto. I told him that he'd be accepting a job in New York and was going to write a book (which he had no plans to do at the time). These things, along with many other details that I picked up on during his session, happened exactly as I foresaw, and over the next few years and with further readings, we became friends. He also began to take an interest in my musical talent and saw potential for me to reenter the business. After writing his book, he moved back to Toronto to accept a job at EMI Music Canada.

Because of his belief in the effect of the meditation, and thanks to the independent success of *Journey Through the Chakras,* he invited me to present the CD to all the department heads and the president of the record company at an executive retreat. Realizing that this might not be a particularly receptive audience, I was nervous. But I knew that the CD and the exercises that I was to facilitate after the meditation would work on anyone with an open mind and some degree of receptivity to their intuition. I just hoped that they had open minds!

Eleven out of thirteen executives had success with the exercises during my two-hour presentation, and within a few weeks I had a licensing deal with EMI Music and my CD was released by a multinational record label. In a roundabout way, my original dream of being a recording artist was being delivered to me. I'd followed my intuition every step of the way as I walked my own path of personal authenticity.

Discussions about a follow-up project led to a phone call to Tori Amos's producer, Eric Rosse, and I flew back to L.A. to work on what I believed would be another meditation CD. However, Eric had a very strong hunch that something else was to occur, and he encouraged me to write a few songs with him. I flew back to Canada, conflicted that I'd spent the label's money on a project that they hadn't authorized, but I was proud and excited because something magical was restored to me.

After hearing the songs, EMI promptly sent me back to L.A. to record my first major-label singer/songwriter release entitled *Magdalene's Garden*. I found my old dream board, which I'd kept because I believed it had never yielded its intention. There I was, 14 years later, looking at the symbol of my dream that said "Capitol Records." (EMI Music Canada was called Capitol Records at the time that I made the board.)

Avalon: A Visit to the Magical Past

After *Hand of Fate,* the success of *Journey Through the Chakras,* and the subsequent recording of *Magdalene's Garden,* I was invited to lecture on intuition in different international cities, and a few years ago, I found myself in the U.K. I have a deep affinity for the British Isles, particularly England—it feels as if the very soil calls me to come home, even though I've never lived there. I do know, however, that I'm familiar, comfortable, and spiritually connected with that land.

I was preparing for a lecture in London, and I decided that I'd go to Glastonbury to visit the area called Somerset, in the southwest part of the country. I'd been there once before but was distracted by my companions, and I knew that I had to return alone. Glastonbury is a magical place, significant to many as the legendary burial place of King Arthur. It's also purported to be the site of the first Christian church in Britain, built by Joseph of Arimathaea, as well as the location of the Isle of Avalon, the legendary home of the priestesses of the goddess culture who served in the Druid traditions. Historians and mystics alike have argued over these facts for centuries, but one thing is certain: This place symbolizes a blending of cultures as Christianity merged with the ancient British traditions during the Roman invasion that imposed a violent ending on the old ways.

People flock from all over to feel the magic of the land and its ley lines that crisscross the area. I believe that I'm bound to this land through a connection to the mythical site of Avalon. As I said earlier, I've always identified with its priestesses' symbols, and even as a small child I painted the blue crescent moons on my forehead that would have marked me as one of Avalon's novice priestesses.

≫ ≪

⟫ ⟪

About a month before I left for England, I'd been study-ing Reiki, the Japanese technique of energy healing. My teacher, Angelique, was also one of my clients—a woman I felt an immediate connection to. I sensed that she'd be able to help me with some issues that I was grappling with as a result of doing readings. She was a powerful master healer who helped me manage my energy, which would get depleted from doing readings and leave me exhausted. When she said that she was going to hold a course in Reiki, I decided to study the first two levels with her. I did so more out of curiosity than anything else, but if it would help me clear myself of negative, unwanted influences and energy, so much the better.

At one point in my training, I was supposed to close my eyes and go into a deep meditative state. Instead, I found myself in the grainy light-filled otherworld that I'd come to recognize as powerfully significant when I experienced it during meditation. I'd come to the session in a pair of jeans and a T-shirt, but suddenly I felt as if I were wearing a dark blue scratchy dress. I went from being seated in a circle in Angelique's funky healing room to sitting on a stone wall beside a well. I distinctly remember the pungent smell of the forest as I was surrounded by the sounds of nature and women chanting—not at all like the New Age music being played at Angelique's.

I was aware that I was somewhere else in time, even though I was still present in the room. It was obvious to me that I'd been in this strange yet familiar and ancient place before. I knew the women who were present, although they didn't physically resemble anyone in the room. I specifi-cally recall the smell of the place and the way it evoked a deep longing in my heart. I felt that two of my friends from this life were there. In my vision, I was being initiated into some form of healing, but I rather abruptly came back to "real time" again as the Reiki session ended. I found the experience powerfully moving.

≫⋘

Once I got to Glastonbury, things began to shift in my awareness. I spent some time wandering around, just feeling the energy of the place. It was almost overwhelming and at times made me quite dizzy. I had to breathe very slowly, as it was almost intoxicating to be there, and I needed time to adjust to all the information I was processing. I kept hearing whispers, and I saw buildings that were in reality only ruins. Sometimes I thought I saw people walking, and when I turned to look at them, they were no longer there.

I went for a walk in the Chalice Well gardens alone, surprised that nobody else was there. It was nearly 4 P.M., and the sky appeared as if it might rain at any moment. I came upon the well itself and was profoundly shaken, since it was clearly the exact place that I'd "seen" at Angelique's. I was aware of being familiar with the local geography, knowing where landmarks had been that were now merely rubble, if they still existed at all. As I felt the magic of the place, I was overwhelmed with emotion and longing. It was as if I'd become two people: One was the modern me, while the other was a woman in a different time. I was keenly aware of myself as a Christian, but I was also deeply connected to my other identity as a Druid, worshipping the goddess and nature in the old Earth religion. I sat on the ground for a few moments to collect myself and pray.

As soon as I closed my eyes, I felt a merging of energy inside me, and my skin began to tingle. It was interesting because even though I experienced this combining effect, I was still aware of my "other" self's energy beside me. When I tried to focus on it, the sense of "her" somehow became less clear. I've always found this to be the case with my gift as well—I observe things by *indirect* seeing, never through my five senses or intellect. The key to intuitive vision and "knowing" is to "de-focus" to achieve clarity, which is the exact opposite of what one would think.

I was there for at least an hour praying and meditating. When I wandered out of the garden, the sun began to peek out from behind a giant cloud. I felt transformed somehow, but I was also sad as I pondered the changes that must have occurred as one manner of worshipping the Divine faded to accommodate another.

As I was leaving, I heard my name being called out very loudly. I'd come by myself, so I was startled and looked around to see who it was . . . but there was no one there, except an old man who wasn't looking in my direction. I stood still for a few moments to collect myself. As I breathed in the damp air, I heard a female voice whisper, "Remember me, Colette. Remember me." There was no way for me to discount this truly visceral experience, and once again I was aware that my path as an intuitive was right. I knew that I was supposed to embrace it and use it to serve others. This was very important, as I'd started to imagine that my new recording career was my true life purpose, which would've taken me away from my service as an intuitive.

I went to bed that night and dreamed of another place and time where I knew the ways of the natural world and possessed an understanding of how to tend to, worship, protect, and honor it. It reminded me that I had no right to impose my will on another and that I must always be accountable to my fellow humanity, the God and Goddess, Mother Nature, and the living planet. My affinity with this place was clear to me. I can't explain it except to say that I'd "come home" in some way. Avalon may be a myth to some, but it's very real to me.

The Great Forgetting

When I returned to Canada, there was a lot of fuss and expectation surrounding my upcoming CD release, so I began to slack off in my spiritual work. I was doing readings and promoting my music, but I neglected my traditional practice of daily prayer and meditation. Consequently, I found myself in a blind place of discomfort. I'd put all my efforts into resurrecting my musical career, and my spiritual focus began to slip.

I had a good fright at a dinner held by EMI Music the night before our big national music-awards ceremony. I sat in front of a wine bottle, and for the first time in 15 years, I thought that I might have a drink. I quickly realized that I was in trouble and immediately went home. It was a powerful reminder that without my spiritual life, I was nothing. I'd forgotten my angel and neglected to say thank you at night and ask for help and guidance in the morning. I'd dropped my guard—my ego was running the show, keeping me isolated from my soul, and my personal intuition had been reduced to a hazy buzz in the background of desire.

Again I'd put the false promise of stardom ahead of my service. I realized that in order to move forward I'd have to find a balance between my two callings. I went back to my daily practices and took a good look at myself. I knew that if I wanted to continue on with music, I'd have to let go of my expectations. By surrendering to whatever would happen, I came to understand that I'd already succeeded beyond my dreams. I'd proven to myself that my love of music was real and called to my heart and soul with true integrity, not just ego. I came to believe that I was indeed talented and that the vision I'd had all my life of becoming a singer/songwriter was a valid one.

I manifested every single intention that I'd set out for in this part of my life. But the thing that I wanted most—approval—I had to find inside of me. The true spiritual lesson is that success is a by-product of immersing oneself in inspiration. When you pursue end results as your main goal (such as approval, happiness, money, prestige, or power), your true aspirations will always remain elusive.

Once I had that epiphany, my life started to fall into place again. I enjoyed both my careers, while trying to remember that my spiritual work had to be the priority. Yet although it was an exciting time professionally, my musical career wasn't going as well as my intuitive one. I had to face the fact that I wasn't going to be the wild recording success that I'd imagined, and I again began to struggle with depression. Even though I understood the lesson intellectually, I hadn't yet fully accepted it or integrated it into my heart.

One night I had a dream. I was sitting at the bottom of a huge old gnarled tree in what appeared to be an ancient forest. An odd diaphanous image of an old man with white hair that reached to the ground hovered in front of me. I remember my discomfort and panic because I was in my favorite pajamas, and in my dream state I wondered why I was wearing them in the forest. Did I forget to put my clothes on when I woke up that day?

The old man laughed as if he could read my thoughts (which he could). He said, "You think that you're awake, but in truth you've forgotten yourself, as has all of humanity since the beginning. It is the Great Forgetting—the illusion that you're here to illuminate. Trust your *inner* vision, not what you *want* to envision, and then you may wear your waking clothes. Ask for what is true."

I frequently have dreams and try to pay attention to their messages, but I don't always have a keen recollection of them when I awaken. This time was very different: The old man's words rang clearly and steadily. When I woke up, I wrote a note to myself in my journal to contemplate the dream. I also prayed, asking for a sign to help me better understand its message. I got in my car, turned on the radio, and heard the Rolling Stones singing about not always getting what you want but getting what you need. Then I switched the station to find someone crooning about not forgetting when something is gone, followed by John Lennon singing about people living in harmony. Imagine that!

It hit me as I was driving that the "Great Forgetting" referred to my own sense of identity, the *Me*—my ego that desires what it wants, when it wants it. When I define *Me* as the most important aspect of myself, I forget that there's a higher consciousness, the *I Am,* which is the spiritual part of me that understands the connection to the Higher Power, the universe, and the greater good. I realized that what I desire may not be in the best interest of all concerned, but if I align my wants with my spirit's goal of the highest harmony, then my needs will always be met. I believe that I was given a mission: to help people remember that intuition is our ability to tune in to that connection. The dream really stuck with me . . . it was definitely an "aha" moment.

That afternoon I sat down to draw up another course description for a workshop I was going to put on for my clients on the subject of manifesting and creative visualization. I kept mulling over the words the old man spoke to me about trusting my "inner vision" and not what I "want to envision." I realized that it's important to ask for what's true, not necessarily what I desire. I had an intuitive vision of all the things that I was inspired to do and create, and that was very different from longing for what I wished to happen. Inspiration was the key, as it came from spirit, and although desire could fuel this in the beginning, too much of it was smothering. I saw that to "want to envision" meant that I was imposing my will on the world—I was intellectually imagining what I hoped for, trying to force a physical manifestation that might not be for the highest good of all concerned.

My depression was about my ego desires coercing an outcome. On the other hand, my intuition was the key to aligning with the universe in order to add harmony to the connection in which all of us are unified. It became apparent to me that there was a much bigger purpose to recovering intuition than I'd understood up to that point. I prayed that I would receive a vision showing me the right way for myself. I asked to be free of the "Great Forgetting" so that I might find truth and wear my waking clothes.

><< ><< ><<

Chapter 10

VISION AND INTUITION—
DESTINY OF THE SPIRIT

I kept feeling an inner push to go back to London, although I was exhausted from trying to juggle my two careers. I conducted 90 percent of my readings over the phone, so there was no real reason for me to travel. I actually preferred telephone consultations, as I couldn't be distracted by body language, and I even asked that the client didn't speak at all until the midpoint of the session. Nevertheless, when one of my long-standing clients relocated to London and sent me an invitation, I jumped at the chance to visit.

When I arrived, it was gorgeous and sunny, and I was thrilled to be back. Things seemed to be going my way. One of my dear friends, world-renowned astrologer Shelley von Strunckel, arranged for me to connect with the Lunar Club, an elite private women's organization that holds monthly dinners featuring guest speakers who lecture on a broad range of spiritual topics. The events were held at the exclusive Sloane Club in London's tony Chelsea District. Being invited there was an honor, and I accepted. I met some extraordinary women, some of whom have now become close friends.

Another client heard that I was going to be in London and contacted the editor of the international magazine *W*. Since, coincidentally, the editor was also coming to London, my client arranged for me to have an interview with him. I was very nervous and spent an hour or so rehearsing what I'd say in my head, trying to remember to stress certain key points. At the time, I was adamant that I be referred to as an "intuitive" rather than a "psychic," and I was hoping that an article in *W* would help my cause. It was the first time I'd received any international press, so I was excited but apprehensive.

Kevin West, the Paris editor of *W*, turned out to be a bright, intellectual, articulate man who, while open-minded, was clearly not a gushing New Age fan. *W* magazine was also noted for its style of acerbic wit and sharp, gossipy journalism, so I was prepared for a sting or two—but instead, Kevin engaged me in a long, wonderful, intelligent conversation. He was respectful and obviously took me seriously, so when the interview was over, I was content.

I waited with bated breath to see the full-page article published. Excited and hopeful, I opened the magazine's glossy pages and found my story, which was entitled "Psychic Hotline: Telephone Psychic is a Little Bit Hocus-Pocus and a Little Bit Rock 'n' Roll." Perhaps I should have taken a closer look at how forcefully I was affirming what I didn't want! I of all people should have remembered that whatever the mind focuses on activates the Law of Attraction . . . so much for my trying to control what others call me—what we resist persists! Although I wasn't thrilled with the tabloid-style heading, the article was well written, fair, and put me on the fast track to further synchronistic alignments.

More and more people called for my services from different locations around the world, and I found myself in a place of deep introspection. What did this mean for the bigger picture of my life? What was being required of me? How could I serve the universe in a more expansive way? Was it through my music?

I began to ask myself all the same questions that my clients did. At that point, I'd reconciled that I was unlikely to be the female-psychic version of Bono, as much as my imagination savored the fantasy. So I began asking for a vision of the next part my life, and I was given the message that I was to write books. I loved creating songs and poetry, but the idea of a book was daunting. Still, in every meditation I got a clear image of standing on a stage, talking to large groups of people about a book I'd written. I had no idea how any of this would come to pass, so I prayed that I'd be shown the way.

Patience: The Wisdom of "Not Yet"

The *W* magazine article began to generate interest from other media sources. Although I did love the attention, I was unprepared for it and had a lot of intuitive resistance to generating too much exposure.

One day within a few weeks of the article's publication, I received an e-mail from the producer of a very popular TV show, asking if I'd be interested in making an appearance. It was an opportunity to be showcased in front of a huge global audience, which would be beneficial to both my music and intuitive careers. It also happened to be one of my favorite interview shows—I watched it all the time and secretly fantasized about being one of the psychics/intuitives who were guests from time to time.

Initially, I was excited and wanted to make the appearance, but I knew that I ought to pray first to see what my Higher Self would tell me. I asked for a vision of what should come next, expecting an image of me signing autographs (clearly an ego-driven concept) and touring around the world, singing and presenting my ideas about intuition. Instead, I received the message: *Patience . . . not yet. Your ego wants it, but it's not your time.* I was sure that I must have heard wrong, so I prayed again. This time I heard, *Decline the offer graciously.* So I did.

I wasn't ready—I was still very confused and conflicted about the balance between my two paths. I'd never advertised or solicited a client, and I was also terribly concerned that I might dilute the effectiveness of my intuitive work by pushing the music. I also knew deep down that I still needed to reconcile my fears around the idea of my service becoming so public. I was continuing to look for outside approval, so obviously I wasn't in a clear place. As much as it disturbed me to say no to the exposure and all its potential, it was the right thing to do.

Fate Fast-Tracks

A few months later, it was time to refocus on my work in both intuition and music, and I got ready to record another CD for EMI. It was called *I Am/Grace,* a two-CD set consisting of seven songs on one disc and an accompanying meditation on the other. I found a wonderful partnership with the award-winning Canadian production duo Boomtang, and I immersed myself in songwriting.

Each song reflected a different aspect of my spiritual experience and perspective expressed in poetic terms that could be applied to the listener's own life. My music spoke of our relationship with God and the different levels of awakening to consciousness. This project gave me such fulfillment, and I'm still very proud of it and its essence. It was a wonderful time: I was busy doing readings, holding workshops every couple of months, and being creative.

At the same time, I was introduced to the man I'd been waiting for all my life—my partner, Marc. We met on a blind date in a bookstore and have never been apart since that day. He had all the aspects I had envisioned in a soul mate: integrity, honesty, trustworthiness, open-mindedness, a deep sense of spirituality, creativity, and a kooky sense of humor—plus, he was pretty darn handsome! Oh, and I forgot to mention that my dog also had to adore him, since we were a package deal. No problem . . . she fell in love with him, too! An extremely supportive man, Marc made it possible for me to take another step forward on my path. Finally, my world was stable and complete for the next ride on the roller coaster.

Through a number of synchronistic connections in London, I was put in touch with a woman named Tessa Graham, the director of a new international brand-management company called Fresh Partners, which was a subsidiary of British celebrity chef Jamie Oliver's company. Tessa and I arranged a phone call a few months after the *W* magazine article. Our conversation is a complete blur in my memory, but her voice and energy made me feel that I'd known her all my life, and she felt the same way. I told her about my desire to write a book and add my voice to those of other wonderful authors and teachers who were helping create a place in popular culture where all things related to the sixth sense could become an accepted every-day experience. She was intrigued, and we decided to meet a few months later.

Our meeting yielded the decision to move forward—and with Tessa at the helm, my proverbial boat set sail. It took about a year for me to really focus on what I wanted to write about. I had to revisit many of the teachings that I'd incorporated into my own work and ask myself some very important questions concerning how serious I was about the commitment I'd be making to my path. I also needed help focusing on the subject of my first book, because I had at least six in mind. One of my clients, a freelance editor named Janice, kept popping up in my mind, and I called her.

Janice and I had had an uncanny experience when we'd first met some ten years before: I'd told her that she was pregnant before she even knew it herself. We had a very strong psychic connection, so it was auspicious for us both that she just happened to have time on her hands to help me with the book. As a gift, I did a reading for her and saw that she'd be hired as a senior editor for a publishing house just days after my project was finished. We laughed and said that we'd better hurry up because her new job was coming . . . and in the end that was exactly what happened!

Over the next four months, we met once or twice a week and finally sent the manuscript for this book to Tessa in London. Tessa oversaw the wonderful presentation package that was ready just in time for the London Book Fair. Many meetings were held, and we received genuine interest from a number of publishers, the obvious fit being Hay House.

Billboards from God

I've always believed that when I'm on the right path, I'll receive some kind of sign. My guides, angels, and God all get together and send me "billboards" when they really want to get my attention. It's been like that most of my life . . . it's as if the universe has to yell at me before I notice where I am. Given the number of incredible epiphanies I've had through spirit, which resulted in the total transformation of my life—from a broken, suicidal, alcoholic, and emotionally and spiritually bankrupt existence to one of grace, integrity, self-acceptance, healing, and service—I'd say that I pay better attention nowadays!

I was invited to fly to San Diego to meet with the president and CEO of Hay House, Reid Tracy. Even though it felt right, I still wasn't sure if it really was, or if I just *wanted* it to be right. I asked for a sign when I stepped on the plane—and instead of just one, I got many!

First, I was seated next to a mother holding a baby with a very uncommon appearance—he was blond, with arresting bright blue-green eyes and Asian features. He looked like an angel from another galaxy, and even his energy was almost otherworldly, as if he were an ancient man inside a teeny infant's body. I struck up a conversation with his mom, and she said that he was unusually calm and quiet this flight. He kept watching me, staring directly into my eyes.

I don't know at what point in our conversation we began talking about aging, but I asked if I could touch the baby's skin, which looked so soft. I compared it with my own, which was showing the signs of my 47 years. Suddenly, the little baby swung around and bent over to caress my hand, looking up directly into my eyes—it was as if I were seeing a real angel. I heard in my mind, *This is illusion. You are always forever. Always.*

I was flabbergasted, and his mom exclaimed, "He never does that! He never interacts with strangers! Wait until I tell his father!" She held her baby up over her shoulder, and as he rested his head on it, he looked squarely at me and winked. No way could I miss that! That was billboard number one.

When I arrived in San Diego, I was met by a well-groomed African-American man who politely asked if he might carry my bags to the limo that was waiting for me outside. I said yes and asked him if he'd be willing to take me to a Coffee Bean & Tea Leaf so that I could get my favorite sugar-free coffee drink—a ritual for me whenever I arrive in California. He was very polite and accommodating, and we began to chat. At some point in the conversation, he identified himself as a born-again Christian. I was curious to hear what he had to say, and we spoke at great length about our beliefs concerning moral responsibility and our relationships to God, the planet, and each other.

Although the way we phrased things was different, I realized that the driver and I were fundamentally agreeing on everything. The light of the seeds that gave rise to all the religions on the planet since the dawn of time shone between us, and it was an exhilarating exchange. Not once did he say that his way was the only one; instead, he spoke of God's world being the path of truth as opposed to ego. There was no talk of ideological differences. We discussed commonalities and the human spirit—not at all what I expected, given my profession.

When we arrived at the stunning, first-class property where I was to stay, this man opened my car door, and with fervor and joy on his face, said, "Behold, the riches of my kingdom will be yours when you do my work and bless my name!" I was stunned. Then there was a bit of a commotion as the bellhop got my attention; seconds later, I turned to thank the driver, but he was gone—I never got his name.

The next day I was to meet with Reid Tracy and then head directly back to the airport. I was calm and happy. I'd met with other publishers, so I wasn't 100 percent sure I'd walk away with a book deal, but I certainly knew that something magical was happening.

Miracle in the Morning

The next morning I went to the lobby and was greeted by a particularly beautiful girl named Roxanne who told me that she'd arrived to take me to Hay House. She was polished on the outside: perfect hair, flawless makeup, naturally gorgeous, and (of course) wearing fashionable clothes. She looked like she had it all together. She held out her hand in a professional manner, and as soon as she touched me, I was overwhelmed with a "knowing" that she was in trouble.

My intuitive radar was on overload. I knew that I should buy some time, so I asked her to drive me to get a coffee before my appointment. I wasn't sure how I'd approach her, but I could feel her suffering as if it were my own. I knew the generational legacy of alcoholism—I was a living example of it myself, and I could always spot it in my work as an intuitive. In my head, I saw her mother drinking and suffering in isolation. I saw Roxanne drunk on a Saturday night, having a blackout. I knew that she was lost and that no one who tried to help her could reach her. I saw the potential for the degraded and demoralizing life of a female alcoholic—like the one I'd once led.

I decided to break my rule of never giving unsolicited readings (which I strongly feel can be both intrusive and awkward). I said, "I hope it's okay to say so, but I keep sensing that your mother is an alcoholic." She was flabbergasted, as she'd never received a reading from any other author. She said that she avoided them but was open to hearing what I saw around her.

As we drove to the Hay House office building, I revealed personal things about Roxanne, her family, and her circumstances. My intuitive gift of clairvoyance was going full throttle as I watched her life like a movie in my head and told her what I was witnessing.

As we pulled in to the parking lot, I knew that I'd be late for the appointment, but the book deal didn't seem very important to me at that moment. It felt as if I'd come to San Diego for this woman. We sat for a good long time while she cried and told me about her pain, and I shared my own and how I overcame it. I could feel her resolve teetering, and I decided that I wouldn't leave the car until I knew for certain that the message had been carried to her. When I could feel the click of spiritual connection in my heart, I went inside for the meeting.

When Spirit moves us to perform selfless service, time stands still and obstacles move away as we're bathed in the light of the Creator. The truth is that we're all intrinsically and forever connected through our very essence. Intuition informs us constantly, reminding us of this fact. Because of it, Roxanne and I brought forth the spiritual connection of the *I Am* presence that each of us carried within. To my knowledge, she went for help and has never picked up a drink since that day—but instead, has been leading a spiritually centered, sober life.

I may have been late for my meeting, but I was just in time for something else. As for what happened after that day—well, you have the result in your hands. This book is the personal legacy of my experience of recovering my intuition. I share my own story with you as an example so that you may also find *your* connection to the light.

※※ ※※ ※※

PART II

THE PROCESS AND PRACTICE OF RECOVERING YOUR OWN INTUITION

Chapter 11

THE PATH TO
RECOVERING INTUITION

Now that you've had a glimpse of my story, you might feel that you identify with most or even just a little of it—or perhaps you have some questions about how it applies to you at all. So in this part of the book, I'm going to explain intuition, its mechanics, and its greater meaning. I'll give you step-by-step suggestions as to how to recover and further develop your own innate gift. And I'll share what I've come to know and understand, along with what still remains a mystery to me.

Recovering intuition has a purpose beyond simply gaining an advantage in life through increased access to information. Of course by combining it with our other five senses and intellect, we do indeed expand our awareness, and our impact on the world becomes greater. Yet our sixth sense extends past our personal boundaries, beyond the sensory, individual consciousness of *Me,* to include much more. I want to help you recover your intuitive gift—but not just to show you how to find the perfect parking spot or protect yourself from personal harm . . . it's way bigger than that.

The greatest gift that I've received from my sixth sense is hope. You see, intuition isn't just a forgotten sense that's grown rusty from disuse or been shut down due to ignorance and a lack of understanding—although these things are indeed true. I invite you to consider the implications of its ability to extend us beyond the limitation of our *selves*. Its greatest gift to us (if we're willing to accept the concept) is *limitless connection*. It reminds us that separation is an illusion of perception.

Even advances in science have proven that we're all made up of a substance that's ultimately intelligent and unified, separated only to form unique expressions of itself. Connection is about unity, a "collective consciousness." Once such wholeness is experienced, we're able to know firsthand what all the wisdom teachers, great prophets, and philosophers have spoken about since the beginning of time. When we truly experience transcendence from self—from our identification with form, or *Me*—we find ourselves linked to the source of all: Divine consciousness. All my epiphanies and psychic/intuitive experiences have shown me that the connection to this creative light, love, universal consciousness, "All-That-Is," God, Divinity, Spirit—whatever you choose to call it—is by any name undeniable and true.

As intuition brings awareness to each of us, it becomes contagious, as one by one we share our awakened state of connection. As we become aware, we understand that to despise another person is to hate ourselves, and to love and support someone else reflects back onto us. In a nutshell, the world becomes a better place—this is the true power of awakening and recovering the sixth sense. So if you're still looking for an important reason to develop this innate gift, think of it as something that will ultimately serve the survival of our species. (And, yes, intuition *will* help you know who's on the line without caller ID.)

When I say that intuition is there to remind us of our limitless connection, it means that we're responsible for this gift because we *are* our intuition—we comprise the substance of that six-sensory connection. Our bodies, minds, souls, memories, past lives, and the helpers surrounding us in the world of spirit are part of this unity that makes up life.

By developing your intuition, *Me* organically becomes *We*—but not the *We* that's comprised of a group of individual *Mes*. The five senses give us the illusion of a smaller universe centered on the *self* . . . the experience of *Me*. Our sixth sense, in contrast, constantly reminds us that we can and should expand our awareness outward into this vast, limitless unified consciousness, which I refer to as the Divine presence of *I Am*.

We find, in exploring this, a profound spiritual truth. We are *not* containers for the soul. We actually live *inside* it, and are made of it, even though we're not always conscious of it. This is how we're united and connected. This is how the ability and awareness of the sixth sense connects to all of life and its possibilities.

As you take the step forward to explore yourself and recover this magical, extraordinary ability that's been given to every human being, remember to reflect on the fact that intuition is something we're all capable of finding and using. It's a gift that allows us to reach far beyond our personal, limited perception of reality; it reminds us that we're forever connected. "Remembering" intuition uncovers our true sense of spirituality as we contemplate ourselves within this boundless unity. Most important, intuition helps give us a new sense of meaning as we tap in to our soul—and this, in turn, reveals the truth: that the spiritual world exists with no borders to divide us.

≫≪ ≫≪ ≫≪

Chapter 12

HOW INTUITION WORKS

Intuition is the sixth sense that everybody possesses, although it varies in degree from person to person. It can best be described as an illogical sensory experience that comes from a location outside of personal awareness and temporal reality. The five senses—taste, touch, smell, hearing, and sight—depend on the physical body and your own consciousness. Everything is relative to you in the moment of experience, so it's safe to say that these senses operate within the confines of linear time. For example, you see this book *now,* not *yesterday; y*ou touch the fur on your dog's head *now,* not *tomorrow.*

The personal consciousness of time is important to mention right away because the mind is like a computer that stores every five-sensory experience you've ever had, creating individual memories that relate to the past. All that you've learned intellectually or felt emotionally is housed there, too. Your unique personal awareness is governed by memory, as well as by the automatic intelligence inside you that makes your heart beat, your skin sensitive to touch, your nose smell, and so forth.

Everyone believes that he or she is an individual with a unique personality, operating under the personal identity called *Me*. *My* memories, *my* knowledge, *my* emotions, *my* identity, *my* preferences are some examples of what helps make up the definition of self, which then dictates our moment-to-moment personal experience.

Our intuition, however, operates outside these limits. Here are some common, everyday examples of when it does:

- The phone rings and you have a flash in your mind—a name or a face—accompanied by the spontaneous insight that a friend you haven't spoken to in years is calling. You answer and it's your long-lost pal. (How could you have logically known this?)

- You have an urge to make a right-hand turn, although the directions you were given clearly tell you to turn left. You later see on the news that you avoided a terrible accident by going the other way. (What made you ignore the directions you were given?)

- You walk into a party and meet a man who's charming and charismatic, yet you feel really nervous around him and dislike him immediately. You find out later that he has a history of abusing women. (You'd never met him before, so what made you feel that way?)

- You're in a great mood, but when you sit down at a business meeting, you're suddenly overwhelmed with sadness. You find out that the person who'd just been sitting in your chair had to put his dog down that morning. (What made you tap in to that sorrow?)

- You know when someone is lying to you on the phone even though you can't see his or her face. (How did you detect this?)

- A feeling that something bad has happened overwhelms you, and you know that your child has been hurt at school. Then you get the call from a teacher confirming your suspicions. (How does that happen?)

- You experience déjà vu—as if you're reliving the moment you're in for the second time—and you know without a doubt what will happen next. (How do you explain this?)

- You're late for a job interview, yet something inside you tells you to linger for a moment in front of a store window. The next thing you know, a really important person shows up and offers you the best job of your life. (What made you risk being late for your interview?)

Experiences like these happen to people every day and are generally said to be lucky coincidences or hunches, or are simply discounted altogether. However, these are really just examples of our intuition informing us of things outside our personal *Me* reality. As these situations illustrate, intuition gives us access to spontaneous bursts of knowledge and insight from beyond our conscious awareness.

Somewhere Else—Local and Nonlocal Reality

Let's assume that "local reality" is like a bubble that surrounds us, defined by the intimate world of the five senses and the consciousness of *Me*. We all have our limits and boundaries that extend from the surface of the bubble inward to include every experience we've ever had or are currently having . . . this is our *perception* of reality. Remember that science has proven that everything is energy—we're made of it and are part of it. Any perceived separation is an illusion. We live and experience this *illusion of separation* in our bubbles because we're built that way.

Many spiritual teachings tell us that we're made unique and individual so that Divine consciousness can be expressed in a multitude of ways. Our very presence and ability to create is a testament to that fact. The illusion of separateness happens when we come to see our finite, individualized form as the sole reality—with a beginning (birth), middle (life), and end (physical death)—forgetting our true limitless spiritual nature. Remember that the presence of *I Am* can only be accessed when we release the attachment to the identity of the *Me* form.

By recovering our intuition, we naturally drop the tight boundaries that separate us as we become receptive to hearing the whispers of the soul. Many of us have had spiritual awakenings triggered by intuitive "aha" moments that broke the bubble open to expose the sparkling, limitless vista of the Divine. We inevitably come back from this temporary enlightened state to do some serious soul-searching and "bubble clearing." Of course, by now you've figured out that the ego, or *Me,* is what lives in the local reality of the bubble.

So *local* reality is what you know and sense directly, while *nonlocal* reality is the unlimited space filled with information that's essentially outside the bubble. It includes other people's memories, emotions, experiences, and events that have an impact on you—knowledge about details and occurrences that have nothing to do with your personal bubble. Nonlocal reality doesn't operate in the context of measured time and space in the same way that the inside of your bubble does: Past, present, and future exist simultaneously. When we tune in to this, we experience another reality that's somewhere else and not local to our individual bubble.

Here's another analogy: Intuition is like a radio that picks up transmissions from a vast cosmic radio station—a living consciousness that's sending out news of everything that's happened, is happening, and will (or potentially could) happen to everything and anyone. It's "out there," and we experience it by receiving it . . . we get the information by tuning in. We allow the boundaries of *Me* to include *more than Me,* sometimes just for seconds, and we intuitively hear this information (clairaudience). Alternatively, it might translate into spontaneous knowing (claircognizance), emotional sensing (clairsentience), or an inner vision or prescient seeing (clairvoyance). I liken it to music that we can hear, experience, and tune in to once we learn how to turn on the receiver.

Natural Development,
Genetics, and Intuitive Activators

So let's assume that we all have intuition. We can all move our bodies, right? But while most of us do so just like everyone else, some individuals are born to go to the Olympics. It's that simple. So there are always going to be extra-sensitive people who have personal bubbles with thinner membranes that are able to stretch and collect all kinds of odd and wonderful information from the unseen world. Let's face it—some people are great at mathematics and other left-brain activity, while others are creative types who are more in touch with right-brain intuitive functioning. However, no matter what level of developmental proficiency we start at, our intuitive ability can easily be honed and expanded.

Most people who are more naturally developed in this area have an obvious aptitude for intuitive reception in one or more sensory areas. For example, I have a client who receives intuitive information by "hearing" things on the right side of her body. She describes this ability as a spontaneous and fragmented inner discussion, which is accompanied by a buzzing sound around her head when she receives intuitive "hits." Another friend of mine, Toronto psychic Kim White, says that she gets energy that runs through her skin and tingles all over when she knows she's on target with what she sees. And after about a year of practicing a guided-imagery chakra meditation that I'd created, one of my students started seeing flashing visions in her head, which was like watching an internal movie of events that didn't belong to her.

When sitting with a client for a reading, I've also experienced a combination of claircognizance and clairvoyance, particularly with regard to past events. But when I'm having a particularly "on" day, it's as if I'm watching a 3-D TV show of my client's life. I've also been in many situations that have affected me physically in which I experienced a heightened sense of awareness—much like a rush of adrenaline—where all six senses appear to be acutely tuned.

Having been exposed to approximately 20,000 different people over the years, I find myself in a position to make some observations. Many of the individuals who shared their stories of unusual intuitive happenings with me mentioned that it ran in their families. They claimed that they had a genetic predisposition to the gift, even if it was kept a secret. In many cases, strong religious superstitions or fears surrounding intuition and psychic phenomena made it much more difficult to live with. People are often afraid of venturing too far outside their personal bubbles, dreading the thought of others intruding on or accessing their private space.

In the 17 years that I've been giving readings, I've also encountered something extraordinary that's common among rape, incest, and other abuse survivors. I mentioned earlier that my ability to access a "witness place" where I can intuit clearly and with detachment, dissociated from my personal identity, was something that came to me during my rape. When I did readings for women (as well as some men) with histories of personal trauma, I found that they shared similar intuitive experiences.

Invariably, all of them developed their psychic or intuitive abilities during and after their traumas. They seemed to become more open to their sixth sense, although most of them didn't understand exactly what they were experiencing. I'd often hear them say, "I feel too much. I sense things in my stomach, and then they happen. I have dreams that come true. I can always tell how someone else is feeling . . . even if they're saying one thing, I know they mean another."

I've found that these people have enhanced intuitive capabilities as a result of the hypervigilance that they subconsciously developed as a means of protecting themselves. Many have claimed that they feel as though they're constantly on patrol, with eyes in the back of their heads—always "feeling out" the spaces around them for things that are hidden, unspoken, and unseen. This increased awareness kept them on the ball, so to speak; however, paradoxically, in their efforts to safeguard themselves, they inadvertently lowered their shields. This resulted in greater access to their natural intuitive birthright, although it also rendered them more emotionally vulnerable.

This legacy among survivors continues to fascinate me as I see it repeatedly manifest itself. In my intuitive-development seminars, the quickest students, as well as the ones who had the most profound experiences, were often those who shared this kind of history. I found the same thing to be the case with people who've encountered near-death experiences: They develop a heightened sensitivity to receiving intuitive information after their recovery. What a price to pay for an ability that's innately available to all of us!

However, this is not the norm, and a traumatic jolt to the psyche doesn't give you a clear, permanent access card to the world of the unseen. Intuitive activators can be as simple as playing music, concentrating on breathing, staring at a lake, praying and meditating, or engaging in a radical sense of forgiveness toward someone who's harmed you. (There are other methods that I'll discuss a little later.) Clearly, there are many gentler and kinder ways of opening up our bubbles to share in the collective bounty of the creative All-That-Is.

≫≪ ≫≪ ≫≪

Chapter 13

WHAT BLOCKS INTUITION?

Each of us has a filter through which we individually decipher six-sensory information. We first receive intuition in the initial flash of knowledge that somehow breaks through our personal bubble. We then translate this information through the filter of our life experiences and personalities, since we've defined ourselves as separate entities.

When we forget our true spiritual natures and identify predominantly with form, we can't help but remain in our bubbles until we're able to transcend them. Everything we've experienced is patterned into this filter that can distort the information that's received, since it's part of the human condition to put everything into form. This is the domain of the ego, the *Me* bubble that can only work with the five senses—but intuition tunes us in to the nonlocal reality outside of this limited perception. Our ego uses the bubble to create a sense of separation in an attempt to maintain a unique *Me* identity, and this is what blocks intuition.

Here's an example: You resent someone whom you believe has wronged you. The expression "nursing a grievance" conjures up an image of holding a baby and feeding it your life force in order to keep it alive. You may not be aware of this all the time, but your resentment is always influencing you. Think of it as a radio that's constantly projecting a jumble of ugly sounds into the airwaves of your mind. How are you going to tune in to the sound of your intuitive voice with all that noise going on?

Try it yourself by revisiting a former grudge or calling to mind one that you may currently be holding. How does it feel? Notice the sense of constraint around your chest and throat. You feel cut off, right? What sensation do you experience in your heart? Do you feel open with love and compassion or closed down with anger and fear? Negative emotions keep us trapped inside our bubbles, cutting us off from our true spiritual natures and binding us to our egos.

The Goblin

I have a nickname for the negative chatter in our minds that keeps us addicted to defining our experience by the form of the bubble—I call it the "Goblin." This is how we miss the opportunities pointed out to us by our intuition.

The Goblin lives inside every human being and is the manifestation of an unhealthy, wounded ego. It's fed by our thoughts of resentment, anger, fear, shame, guilt, sloth, envy, indifference, competition, greed, lust, and every other expression of lack and limitation. The Goblin is in charge of keeping us in "separation mode" and would just love it if our personal bubbles were made of fortified steel so that we'd never have a glimpse into our limitless connection.

The Goblin depends on the concept of separation to maintain a unique *Me* identity.

If we transcend this perception, the Goblin has no identity or purpose and dies or falls into a deep sleep. Therefore, it has a vested interest in keeping us in our bubbles and shutting down anything that reminds us of another reality. The Goblin keeps the filter clogged on purpose so that it remains the false center of the universe inside the bubble. The Goblin continuously repeats a song to itself that goes, "Me-Me-Me-Me-Me"—and that's the music we hear much of the time.

The Goblin is a clever little creature that keeps our focus on distracting, persistent, and loud noise. It wants us to believe that it's who we are—that its thoughts are ours—and the only identity that matters is its own. The Goblin is in the bubble of local reality and has no connection to anything on the outside because it only has the capacity to see itself. So it's safe to say that the Goblin is the worst part of our personal identities.

When the sixth sense tunes us in to a nonlocal reality that threatens to pop the bubble, it causes the downfall of the Goblin. Remember the Wizard of Oz? He was a fraud, and everyone found out that he was just a little chubby man behind a curtain, manipulating people into thinking that he was the all-powerful center of an entire land. The Goblin is an imposter, too, because it wants us to believe something that's only an illusion.

Be aware that the Goblin has a vested interest in keeping us in a five-sensory universe because it will lose its power if we see through different eyes or hear with another pair of ears. I'm repeating these concepts so that you see how the Goblin affects your reception of intuitive information. Our natural human mind-body-spirit mechanics equip us with a sixth sense, our special radio that receives information before it gets filtered. The radio waves are invisible but always exist in an unlimited supply. The music of the cosmos beams into our receivers, but the Goblin plays with the dial and purposely tunes it to the wrong station.

Have you ever been in a car with a bratty little kid? You might decide to turn on a children's CD in order to keep him quiet. Even though you're trying not to pay attention, you still have to listen to it, and later those same songs remain stuck in your head, perpetually repeating themselves. Your Goblin is like that unruly child, and you're listening to the station that plays the tunes that your Goblin loves to hear over and over. Without even realizing it, a lot of the time you hear:

> *You're listening to Goblin Radio EGO-FM, the home of suffering and fear! Tune in for our special guest, the CEO of Financial Insecurity, followed by Miss Grandiosity and her little sister, Never Enough, singing their hit songs, "More and More" and "Gimme Yours."*

How do you change the station to allow greater personal access to your intuition? Like the bratty kid, the Goblin really just needs a nap! When it's asleep, an awakening of your Higher Self takes place, and you find less blocking your path. You also develop greater natural access to your intuition and can learn how to tune in to a completely different station.

The Conversation for Transformation— Getting to Know the Goblin

To begin the process of recovering your innate gift of intuition, it's crucial that you become conscious of how you perceive the world. How much are you in your bubble? How tight is your hold on defining your world through your five senses and logic? You know that there's more, so how do you bring your local reality into balance with the cosmos? How do you quiet the Goblin and lessen the damage caused by always perceiving separation?

The following exercise will help you begin the process of transformation, providing you with an instant lullaby for your inner Goblin. Use it whenever you're feeling stressed, agitated, fearful, angry, or resentful. It will help you release your wounded ego and restore inner balance so that your intuition isn't blocked. This exercise will also let you build an imaginative and creative relationship with your inner Goblin. Have fun with it, and you'll be amazed by how different you feel afterward!

1. First, put on some meditation music that you really love—preferably with sounds of the ocean or trickling water, as these provide a natural relaxation effect.

2. Sit comfortably in a chair and breathe deeply for about 15 counts. Allow all the tension you're holding in your muscles to release, relaxing your body as best you can.

3. Imagine that you're alone, sitting in the audience of a theater and looking up at a stage that's flanked by a heavy curtain. Behind it is your Goblin, the part of you that's expressing the difficult emotion (such as fear, anxiety, or anger).

4. Invite this part of you to come out from behind the curtain and show itself to you in the form of some kind of character. (You might observe a tiny childlike version of you, a funky little fairy, or something weird such as a fuzzy image of sparkles; however, for the purposes of this exercise, the character will be a Goblin.) Don't panic if you can't see anything. You can still communicate back and forth with an aspect of yourself that will make itself known—but you may feel or hear it, instead of seeing it.

5. Now invite the Goblin to tell you what's on its mind. Let it know that you'll listen to all it has to say. Allow it to rant, emote, stamp its feet, cry, yell, or whatever it wants to do . . . its response will be different every time. It may say nothing, instead sending you mind pictures. However it tries to communicate with you, just hear it out and don't interrupt.

6. When the Goblin has finished, imagine yourself rising from your chair and walking up the stairs leading to the stage. Approach the Goblin and ask it what it needs from you, reassuring it that you're committed to looking after and loving it. Then thank it for sharing its feelings with you.

7. Take a baby blanket and wrap it around the little Goblin. Hold the creature close to your heart, and tell it that with love there's no fear.

8. Next, bring the white light of all the love in the universe through you and into the sleepy Goblin, and experience how you feel as this creature is absorbed into your being, filled with love and peace.

9. Ask yourself who's talking to the Goblin. What part of you is expressing itself as the nurturer? How does it feel to be choosing to look through the eyes of your authentic self—your Soul Self?

10. Be aware that *you* aren't your Goblin's feelings. The Goblin doesn't limit you except by the perception that it imposes upon you. After conversing with it, notice the shift in consciousness as your awareness is restored and balanced and you automatically see through another pair of eyes. Yes, it's that easy!

This exercise is the first step in the process of removing blocks to your intuition. It's been the foundation of my spirit coaching, and I've seen amazing results with everyone who tries it. Remember to keep a journal of your conversations so that you can keep track of the inner transformation that follows.

⇶⇶ ⇶⇶ ⇶⇶

Chapter 14

THE NEXT STEP TO RECOVERING INTUITION

The process outlined in this book relates to recovering and developing a conscious connection to your intuition. It's the path of Divine synchronicity, where preparation meets opportunity and you're guided by your intuition, not your ego. It's about freeing yourself from the bondage of the Goblin within that sabotages you, puts you in competition with others, and makes you feel afraid that nothing you do is ever good enough or that the world doesn't have enough to go around. This process will help you disengage from the self-limiting patterns that keep you from hearing the intuitive messages that point you to your true path.

The process of regaining your intuition is all about ego deflation—lulling your inner Goblin to sleep so that it can't interfere with the magic radio that's tuning you in to the unlimited world of the spirit and the immeasurable, timeless possibility within the All-That-Is. This involves becoming aware of your uniqueness while still recognizing the unity among all humanity. It isn't about applying your sixth sense to get what you want; it's about aligning yourself with a higher purpose and trusting that you'll ultimately be led to the highest good of all.

This process is concerned with the undeniable responsibility that we all have to the rest of the world to be the best we can be on any given day. This means going into your past and blessing and releasing the conditioning that prevents you from moving forward in a healthy, multi-sensory direction. In this way, the future will unfold for you in fullness, beauty, and strength.

Tuning the Intuition Radio— Introducing the 7 Spiritual Keys

Imagine that your intuition radio has preset buttons that were programmed when you were born to link you to the universal cosmic station. When you tune in to the right frequency, the signal is clear and magical. I like to think that we're all preprogrammed to Spirit Radio SOUL-FM, the home of harmony, wisdom, fairness, compassion, respect, and truth—where connection is the only way of being.

When the Goblin gets a hold of your radio, you're either listening directly to EGO-FM or picking up a lot of static because it's interfering with your six-sensory reception as you try to tune in to another station. Often your local awareness has become so limited that you ignore the radio or lose the ability to hear it altogether. People like me receive its signals full blast—but sometimes even I get a lot of static and interference when I try to listen to what it's saying.

Even though some of us hear the station loudly from the get-go, it certainly doesn't mean that we'll have clarity with regard to how we distill the information. Being psychic or highly intuitive doesn't imply that we automatically get special filters. Unfortunately, the ego doesn't care about the connection to the All-That-Is or anything else that might remind it of that limitlessness. If anything, having a wide-open reception to six-sensory information without a strong sense of spirituality, morality, and a healthy balance of intellect and emotion can result in psychological difficulties.

There's a great responsibility resting on the shoulders of the individuals who are called to serve others with their psychic/intuitive awareness. They need to be just as vigilant about their Goblins, if not more so, since others turn to them for help and guidance. So this applies to every one of us if we want to positively contribute to the world.

It's been my experience that engaging in a process of ego deflation will lead directly to a spiritual awakening that organically recovers our innate access to the intuition radio. Not only that, but it cleans the filter and gets the Goblin to take a nap, too . . . one-stop intuition-recovery shopping! I've done the exercises that are part of this process and have made using them a way of life. Once *you* try them, you'll be amazed by how much they help you tune in to your intuition.

There are 7 main Spiritual Keys to tap in to: *Truth, Reverence, Humility, Courage, Forgiveness, Stillness,* and *Love.* When you make them a part of your way of life, you can recover your access to your personal intuition radio. The Keys all lead to connection and serve to reduce the separated sense of self—the ego-centered *Me* bubble. They help dissolve the membrane of the bubble so that it's inclusive of others, life, and God. These important steps will help you prepare to recover your intuition, eliciting a spiritual awakening whereby you'll begin to remember that you are in fact a fully six-sensory being.

Tuning in to these higher frequencies and practicing specific exercises will help remove any blocks to recovering your intuition. Once you've committed to placing yourself on the path, you'll be ready to engage in the exercises that I've outlined, which deal specifically with stretching your awareness into the domain of the sixth sense. That is, I'll show you how to tune in to some very specific intuition-radio programming.

Remember that living intuitively requires balance and the faith that all your gifts come from the Divine. Contemplating the 7 Keys will always bring you into alignment with this concept. And don't forget to have fun with it, too . . . enjoy your journey!

※※ ※※ ※※

Chapter 15

THE 1ST KEY: TRUTH

Who are you? That's a good question, and one that can send all of us down the rabbit hole of quantum physics, psychology, neurophysiology, religion, and existential philosophy to try to find an answer.

To simplify things, we have to start with the dualism that we're actually hoping to transcend. Remember that the fundamental basis for recovering intuition is accessing that limitless connection that exists between all of us. We must also recall that we live and experience ourselves in personal local reality that I call the "*Me* bubble." That said, we can answer the question "Who are you?" in two ways: (1) I am *Me*, and (2) I am *more than Me*. I am also the consciousness of the presence of the *I Am*—as Eckhart Tolle so eloquently describes in his book *A New Earth*, "the Being *behind* the human." This is also referred to as the "Higher Self" or the "consciousness of the soul." It's this emergent awareness that directly engages the intuition by providing us with information and helping us ensure that our filters are clear.

The intuition filter becomes clogged because of the ego's need to only acknowledge local reality as truth. But, in fact, this version of "truth" is limited by the five senses that translate everything around us into a tangible, measurable, materialistic reality. So "Who are you?" can in part be answered with "I am everything that is *Me*—an accumulation of experience and learning, from birth until now."

Simply put, being *Me* is about living in a story. Objectively getting to know *your* story, including what's influenced it and why, will help you clear your filter. It's like taking an inventory of everything in your house and knowing where each item is. If you trip on something, you don't ask, "What's that?"; rather, you know that you bumped into a box labeled "My Unresolved Stuff with Dad" or "My Childhood Memories." You're also aware that you own everything in your house.

So the 1st Key is about shining a bright light on yourself, which is the beginning of freedom from the bondage of *Me* (and your Goblin). In addition to what's easily and willingly revealed through self-reflection, you also shed this illumination directly onto your shadow.

Exploring Your Story

As you explore your story, keep in mind that even though everything in it is in the past, it informs your present, consciously or unconsciously. And if you gauge your awareness of yourself on a scale that moves from the negative elements of separation (including isolation and divisiveness) to the more positive ones (evolving toward the knowledge that you're a unique expression of Divine consciousness), you'll find some interesting things. You're going to be somewhere between (a) totally self-centered and narcissistic and (b) fully engaged in celebrating unity within diversity.

It doesn't matter where you start from, as this isn't an inventory of how "good" or "bad" you are. Instead, it's an exploration of *who* you are and what you believe about yourself in the world—it's a fact-finding expedition. It's really important to know who you are and what you'll be dealing with as you embark on expanding your awareness outside the bubble.

The identity of *Me* is also defined and served by what gets expressed and communicated between yourself and other people. The act of telling the truth about who you are to yourself and others is hugely important because it results in clarity, which is essential if you want to tune in to a greater awareness. Being honest feels powerful, grounded, freeing, and real. Conversely, denial and telling outright lies to someone in an effort to manipulate, control, and obtain what you want is the Goblin's territory. Denial is that damaging way you deceive yourself—for example, the psychological delusion inherent in the diseases of alcoholism and addiction or in the refusal to accept that your partner is cheating on you. Lying feels a little like being drunk: It make you falsely elated (you think that you've gotten away with something) but also fearful, tense, ungrounded, and unreal.

Intuition feels the same as the truth: It might not make sense logically or intellectually, and the five-sensory body may not grasp it, but when you initially tune in to it, it seems as real as anything in the bubble. It's only after you filter it that it can get distorted, because although it may lead to information about the bubble experience, it doesn't belong within it or obey its laws. This is an important point that I'll be repeating in order to reinforce it.

Remember that intuition is information from nonlocal reality that can be applied to inform what is going on, has gone on, or could go on in the bubble or in the universe at large. Always be aware of the things that you're feeling, since wishful thinking is occasionally disguised as intuition. Sometimes when you think that you're objectively checking in with yourself, it still feels like lying—and that's because it is.

Exploring the Truth and the Identity of Me

Acquainting yourself with *Me* is the first and most important endeavor you'll undertake in this book. It requires as much honesty as you can muster, since you'll be doing an inventory of your personal life story and how it informs your present. The purpose of this is to demonstrate how you see yourself as a separate being and to recognize self-limiting patterns that keep your personal intuition filter clogged. Since the whole process of recovering intuition is about freeing oneself from ego bondage, lulling the Goblin to sleep, and then tuning in to a higher personal frequency that's not burdened by the unresolved content of *Me,* this section should be done first before attempting to move on. The bottom line is that in order to tune in to your intuition, you need to know the true content of the world that exists in the mind of *Me.*

You'll need a journal for this exercise. Keep it separate, only writing specifically about yourself, how you've related to others, and the way you've been influenced by everything that pertains to you. It's a good opportunity to begin to honor this expansive process, so buy yourself a journal that's really special, such as a leather-bound one, or perhaps make one yourself, decorating it with images that you cherish. This volume will constantly evolve as you find out new things about yourself. Over time you'll even see how you can rewrite your personal history as your perception changes and you contemplate the rest of the Keys.

Let's get started. . . .

1. Write your life story starting from your first memory, listing the most pertinent events in chronological order. Try to be objective—just record the facts.

2. Now write your story in relation to your parents, siblings, and other relatives, in an effort to understand the dynamics within your family.

3. Jot down as much as you know about your grandparents and your ancestors. If your parents are still alive, ask them to tell you as much as they know and include that information.

4. Write your life story from the perspective of how you were wounded. (It could be by anyone, including parents, boyfriends, girlfriends, creditors, yourself, and so on.) This helps you see how you may unconsciously be playing out the role of victim in your life and recognize patterns within relationships.

5. Now rewrite the same story, this time from the perspective of what was good in your life. (For example, instead of saying how your mother was critical, talk about how she made you delicious meals and kissed you good night; rather than stating how you hated going to school, talk about how you loved recess.) The aim is to show you how to change your perception.

6. Ask yourself, *Which of the stories I listed are true?* Then note how that truth is serving you and why.

7. Write a list of spontaneous statements that start with "I believe . . ."; then record *why* you believe those statements.

8. Compile a list of every memory you have of lying to someone else. Now make another one for when others have lied to you.

9. Close your eyes and tell yourself three things that are absolutely true. Write them down, and notice how you feel physically and emotionally when you tell the truth. Now say three total lies out loud and write them down, noting how it feels to do so. Record the differences between the two experiences.

10. On a separate page, draw a bubble. Write the question "Who are you?" above it and the word *Me* in the center. What would you put within this space? What describes the experience of the bubble? Then add words inside the bubble to answer the question "Who are you?" Be sure to include positive and negative experiences and emotional descriptors.

This is a fun, ongoing exercise. As you continue with the rest of the Keys and development tools, you'll want to create new bubble drawings, since you'll begin to see how much your personal truth can be altered over time. You should now be aware of what's contained in the *Me* bubble, which allows you to remain conscious of your patterns and other personal identity markers. Even seemingly simple and innocuous things such as likes and dislikes may bias the perspective of your experience.

Exploring More Than Me

Once again, it's time to answer the question "Who are you?" Let's now explore: "I am *more than Me.*"

1. Sit comfortably in a chair and close your eyes.

2. Bring your attention to the outside of your body and become aware of your physical impressions of five-sensory information. Write down what you experience.

3. Turn your awareness inward, and observe your emotions. How do you feel? Emotions are usually ephemeral, but see if you can get a general idea of what's going on in your heart. Jot down what you feel.

4. Now observe your thoughts for a while. What are you thinking about? Is there any particular pattern? If not, what's randomly going through your mind? Are you analyzing something, or are you just all over the place, contemplating nonspecific things? Note whatever comes to mind without judgment.

5. Become aware of the aspect of you that's making these observations. Remain in this experience for a few minutes (or as long as you can—it gets easier with practice).

6. Now "observe the observer." Try to remain in this perspective as long as you can before writing down the experience. When you do record it, describe it as best you can. Ask yourself, *Who's watching me? Who's watching the one watching me?*

7. On a piece of paper, draw a *Me* bubble, making the line around it clear. Then draw arrows from the bubble to the outer edge of the paper. Everything outside the bubble should be labeled as "The Domain of All-That-Is."

8. Next, draw arrows pointing back into the bubble, "popping" it. Sketch a wavy broken line outside the rim of the bubble to represent this. It should look like a bubble inside a larger one, with a fluid, open boundary that allows the outer realms to naturally perforate it, thereby suggesting its connection to the limitless All-That-Is. Label this "The Transcendent Consciousness of the All-That-Is."

You've now begun to understand and experience the possibility of the second answer (to the question posed at the beginning of this chapter), pointing to the universal spiritual truth: *more than Me.*

>>⋘ >>⋘ >>⋘

Chapter 16

THE 2ND KEY: REVERENCE

Reverence for life and all that it implies is essential in order to stretch us outside our egocentric bubbles and open our reception to the All-That-Is. It leads us to remember that the Divine flows through us and every other living being: "As above, so below."

Reverence is a fundamental respect and empathy for the world around us, along with a sense of awe at its mystery. Intuition taps in to this and reminds us that we as individuals aren't the center of the universe . . . something greater and more profound than we're capable of fully understanding flows through life both in and around us. When we experience reverence, we recognize the Divine power of the creative pulse in all things as we take our place within the diversity of life.

Contemplating this mystery evokes a reverence that can be life altering. On a more humorous note, it's like getting an instant vacuum cleaning of our personal filters, which allows us to be in tune with all of life—its signals and signs, its whispers and omens. Once our filters are cleared, we hear the sounds of the cosmos with clarity, even if only for a brief moment. Reverence makes us wide-open to the possibility of the All-That-Is and keenly receptive to the messages that our sixth sense brings to our experiences.

When I was a little girl, I first felt reverence in church and in the teachings of my Christian faith. I was awed by the stories of the Bible and by the power of the Holy Trinity. The implication of the soul filled me with awe. The possibility of angels and other celestial beings fascinated me.

Because I was fortunate enough to have a father who respected other cultures and religions, I was introduced to his collection of books so that I'd learn about the diverse ways people find to commune with the "mystery." I was again awed by the complex manner in which humankind strove to understand and revere the Divine. Whether describing one god or many, all cultures had the same need to search for meaning.

As I grew up, I was exposed to other experiences that instilled such awe in me. As reverence took hold of me in the jungles of Dominica, I was amazed by the vastness and richly interdependent intricacies of the natural world. Even the experience of watching the seven bright lights that my father said were UFOs gave me a great sense of respect for the extraordinary possibility that life exists beyond what we know. By contemplating this mystery, I felt an open connection to all living things.

Reverence is easy when we're children, as we all have a natural empathy and compassion for everything around us because we aren't yet influenced by the cynicism that accompanies adult existence in the modern world. Thousands of my clients have told me that they felt this wonder as children, but as they grew up and their personalities and life experiences became more complex, the moments of reverence became fewer and fewer. In the rich Western world, the urban phenomenon of going camping—leaving behind the hustle and bustle of the city to relax in a tent by a remote lake—is a means of recapturing a sense of reverence, whether or not there's a conscious awareness of this urge.

In cultures where people have experienced poverty and violent turmoil, this feeling is lost in the killing of life and the hatred that accompanies it—but it can be found again in moments of surrender, when suffering has rendered everyone equal once again. Recognizing the tiniest glimmer of the life force in a blade of grass can open our hearts to the connection among us all, reminding us that each step we take is in a dance with others. As a conscious part of daily life, reverence reminds us of the vastness of the mystery that surrounds us and the respect that we're compelled to give it.

Respect for All Life

When we contemplate the life force around us with awe and respect, we open ourselves up to receive its messages. We sense the intrinsic connection between all living things, and in so doing, it changes us.

I vividly recall a spontaneous moment of reverence that took place in January 1986. It was when I was in treatment for alcoholism and my life was in shambles. I'd been in rehab for a week and was still delusional and totally self-centered, as addicts typically are. The recovery facility was situated directly on a lake, and there was plenty of time to go for walks and contemplate things, so one day I went out alone and decided to go as far around the lake as I could.

There was lots of snow on the ground, but the temperature had risen, and big patches of mud were scattered here and there.

As was typical for me at the time, I walked with my head down (maybe it kept me from seeing beyond myself). I wasn't watching where I was going, and my foot got caught in the mud. I was forced to stay still while I tried to figure out how to pull it out without losing my boot. No one was around, and I saw that I'd wandered a long way from the main building. The air was crisp, and I felt the stillness of the place as I became more aware of my surroundings.

I glanced up and noticed that one tall, bare tree stood on its own in front of me. I was forced by my predicament to look at it and really *see* it. I was overwhelmed with awe at this natural sight, as if I'd never really observed a tree before or understood what it meant. This was nature . . . this was life. I felt the creative impulse of that All-That-Is—the mystery that had been beckoning to me since I was born. I remember taking a deep breath, and the magnitude of this spiritual moment of awakening gently washed over me. I recall a glimpse of limitless connection where I was no longer at the center.

Reverence and Nature

It would be ideal if you were in a position to find a natural setting and spend some time immersed in the outdoors. But no matter where you are—even if you're stuck in the middle of the city—experiencing reverence is easy. Remember that the goal is to open up to the vast potential of the All-That-Is and acknowledge life with reverence. Once this is established as a starting point, it becomes effortless to

allow communication from outside the bubble to permeate your consciousness. You then begin to receive and use
intuitive information with respect.

Most cities are built close to a body of water. Since this
is the element that's most precious to all of life, contemplating its rhythm and very essence is a wondrous way to attain
even just a brief moment of reverence. I'm very fortunate
to live near a beach, and I make it a daily habit to go down
to the water and walk along the shore, contemplating the
magnitude of nature and its mysteries.

Water Exercise

If you can, find a beautiful natural place by water where
you can sit quietly while you do the next exercise. You may
have easy access to one in the form of a river, a brook, or
the sea. If you aren't able to go to such a location, simply
imagine that you're near one. Give yourself about an hour
to complete this exercise.

1. Relax, breathing deeply and allowing your five
    senses to experience the environment. Take in
    the smells, feel the wind on your skin, and notice
    how you feel as you settle into nature.

2. Now pay particular attention to the water, and let
    your busy thoughts melt away as you watch its
    surface. Contemplate the water, its significance to
    life, and its rhythm—be present with it. Then ask
    yourself, *Who or what force or intelligence created
    this water?*

3. Allow yourself to take in the vista and the greatness of its mystery. Make a conscious commitment to honor and respect all living things for their importance to the diversity of life.

4. Contemplate the limitless connection within nature. Think of a prayer of thanks and give it as an offering to the soul of the water.

5. Close your eyes and allow your sixth sense to scan, and tune in to, the surroundings. Write down any messages you may receive in your journal.

You can repeat the same exercise accompanied by symbols of the other elements (earth, fire, or air) as well. The point is to commune with the life force within all of nature.

Flower Exercise

Here's another great exercise for city dwellers, even those who are unable to get to a park or a backyard, since all you have to do is find a favorite bloom to contemplate. It's easy to acquire one—in New York City, for example, vendors sell fresh-cut flowers everywhere.

1. Sit comfortably in a chair, and hold a flower in your hand at the base of its stem.

2. Observe its color, smell, and texture. Ask yourself, *Who or what source created this flower?* Contemplate your answer.

3. Send the flower your deepest respect, and make a
   commitment to honor and value all living things.

This can also be done with a rock, crystal, or any natural substance. The point of this exercise is to help you connect with the life force and Divine intelligence that resides
in all of nature, moving you out of your anthropocentric
perspective. It will also allow you to recognize that all of
life's diverse forms are equally important to the unity of the
whole . . . everything is sacred.

※≪　※≪　※≪

Chapter 17

THE 3RD KEY: HUMILITY

Humility is the place within us that understands that we're not meant to live as isolated islands. It's the recognition of the need for community, showing us our relationship to each other, our interdependence, and our oneness with the All-That-Is. Connection is the domain of intuition and is our reminder that we belong.

Humility asks us to be present in the mystery—in the "not knowing"—and allow our hearts to open so that our response is compassionate, and we're aware of our inherent unity. If we're willing to wait in the dark, the light comes, and we're guided toward the appropriate actions to take to serve our community and family and to indeed find a higher purpose for ourselves. Humility knows that we're required to respond to life on its own terms. We must find strength in the knowledge that we're not alone, that we need, and are responsible for, each other and all life. The statement "You create your own reality" has nothing to do with the will of the ego imposing its desires onto life. It's about becoming aware of and allowing a profound conscious alignment to a higher will. Intuition is the tool of its communication, and humility helps gently activate it.

When we don't see or understand the history of the events in front of us, we need to surrender to *what is* in order to find fortitude. We must reach deep within ourselves to find our connection to the Divine, no matter how unfair life seems to be. Humility can show us miracles when we take our place as one among many.

When we're humble and accept life exactly as it is, our intuition provides us with clarity. Paradoxically, it's in surrendering to this acceptance that we receive the power to change the world, one thought or action at a time. Humility is about knowing that life is tenuous, filled with visible effects originating in invisible causes that are rooted in mysteries we may never unravel. "I don't know" translates to "I'm open to receiving, learning, and sharing."

Opening Yourself Up to Humility

Humility doesn't have to come from humiliation, since it's not necessary to beat us with a stick to make us notice. Instead, it's about gratitude and remembering that everything in our lives is given to us by a Divine Source. Humility entails using our gifts to the best of our abilities; giving thanks for them; and being "other-focused," instead of self-centered. It's also about maintaining a sense of humor, no matter what our lesson may be. It reminds us that every life is a teaching tool for others. Humility is always about living by example and being open and receptive to learning from those around us.

Humility knows that when it's time to "chop wood and carry water," we sometimes spill a whole bucket and have to retrace our steps. We have to be willing to show ourselves fully, including our imperfections and vulnerabilities. Humility means admitting that we're all in this together, and that even though we're each unique (just as no two snowflakes are created alike), we're made of the same stuff—none better or worse. Humility is about accepting the fact that the contrasts and dualities inherent in humanity exist for a purpose. In doing so, we open ourselves to the instruments of power that give breath to our present life. Humility is about surrendering to the illusion and finding the truth, asking for help and acting with compassion and without judgment, remembering that we're here through the grace of God.

Humility is why it's important that I pray every time I do a reading. This is my favorite prayer to say before I begin in order to always remind myself that I'm in bondage to the ego and must release and be lifted to a higher ground so that I may see:

> *God, make me a channel for Divine*
> *clairvoyance and an instrument of Thy peace.*
> *Of myself I am nothing; the Light doeth*
> *the works. Relieve me of the bondage of self*
> *so that I may better hear Your voice*
> *and do Thy will. Let there only be Light.*
> *Show me how I may best serve this person*
> *for the highest good of all concerned.*

When we remember to pray and ask for help and guidance, our intuition rings with clarity because it resonates with the strumming fingers of the Divine, as we seek to be in tune with the cosmos. Humility then becomes a goal rather than an effect caused by struggle and loss of face. It's about asking for help and remembering where the answers come from.

Exercise

In your journal, write the answers to the following questions, giving yourself plenty of time to ponder each in detail. Leave a few blank pages after every one, since you may want to add more thoughts as you move on in the process. It's likely that you'll have new ideas to include as your commitment to the practice of intuition recovery strengthens.

1. What does *humility* mean to you?

2. What are you grateful for?

3. What does it mean to be "one among many"?

4. What's the relationship between pride and humility? Have you ever refused to admit that you didn't know something?

5. What does *service* mean to you? In what areas of your life do you provide service to others? (Explain using five examples.)

6. In what way do you think that human beings need each other?

7. Do you have a hard time asking for help? How does this manifest in your life?

8. What's the nature of giving and receiving? What are some examples of how you give and how you receive? Is one easier than the other?

9. How does the issue of control play out in your life?

10. Why do you think humility is a good principle to strive for as a goal? To what end is humility helpful in your relationship to the world?

11. What is the difference between *Me* and the indwelling *I Am?*

$$\gg\!\!\ll \quad \gg\!\!\ll \quad \gg\!\!\ll$$

Chapter 18

THE 4TH KEY: COURAGE

We need to go beyond the limits of the way we've been conditioned to see the world and how we've defined ourselves if we're to fully embrace the implications of our birthright to multisensory living—where intellect and reason are joined with intuition. Our "radios" are always beckoning us into the mystery of the cosmos so that we'll have another sense of the world and our part in it. We need courage to reach out into the unknown around us as well as face the shadows that dwell within us.

It takes courage to look at and heal the ugly wounds we carry in order to bring those parts of ourselves to light so that we can be freed from their constricting definitions and recover our beauty. Our shadows define us in silence, but speak loudly through us nonetheless—sometimes subtly, sometimes blatantly—turning us into unknowing puppets manipulated by invisible strings.

If we stay within the confines of our local-reality *Me* bubbles, with only the Goblin in charge of our radios, it's easy to forget that we're whole, perfect, and loved. The Goblin tells us that we're all hurt, flawed, wrong, shamed, entitled, and so on. But those wounds need not cause us to define who we are as fragmented and deficient, as they so often do. By perceiving ourselves this way based on our negative experiences, we abdicate our responsibility to release ourselves and become more than we are. It takes courage to remember that the only place where our imperfections mean anything is inside our personal *Me* bubble.

The more we learn about ourselves, the more light shines on us and we're pushed to change. But it takes courage. I don't think we fear failure or the dark as much as our own potential and our quest to reach it. What will happen when we spread our wings and find the winds of the Divine underneath them? It's so much easier to stay in the false security of what we think we know and wait for others to lead first or do the work for us.

Have Courage Now, Not Later

Waiting until the fear subsides, trying to calculate or control the possible outcome from a place of total surety is futile, for a lifetime will pass away before you find your courage. Fear need not be absent for you to listen to the voice pushing you to be brave. By having the inner strength to go beyond your comfort zone, you allow a greater fullness of experience in spite of your fear, as you're pushed by your soul's longing for meaning. This is the incalculable experience of miracles and grace that each of us was born to know.

When I got sober and my gift as an intuitive became undeniable, I was afraid because it wasn't what I'd planned for myself. Yet the more I cleaned up my life, addressed my past, practiced forgiveness, peeled away the layers of my own wounded self, and continued to work on making a deeper conscious contact with God, the more obvious and clear my abilities became. I had to have courage to embrace a calling that was not part of the accepted social norm, when what I wanted most was to belong back in the world as something else.

We're called many times to have courage in our lives, and often we pretend that we don't hear. Who will we be if we're no longer who we were? What, then, will we have to give up? What will we have to change? How can we hold on when what we know is gone and the future is still unseen? It takes great courage to experience the adventure of our complete selves, to look at ourselves with honesty. It requires courage to face our denial and stand naked in the light of our spirits, slowing down long enough to let life slam us, sometimes shattering our frantic lives so that we realize that running at lightning speed hasn't taken us very far. To gather all our fragile parts in our arms as we're called to the edge—after truth, faith, and humility have given us a clear vision—is the gift of this process. To be there at all is the beginning of knowing.

Courage is expressed so beautifully in the following little story adapted from a poem written by Christopher Logue in honor of Guillaume Apollinaire:

He said, "Come to the edge."
I said, "I can't; I'm afraid."
He said, "Come to the edge."
I said, "I can't; I'll fall off."
He said, finally, "Come to the edge."
And I came to the edge.
And he pushed me.
And I flew.

Once we've allowed ourselves to go to the edge, letting go is the only choice we have, and courage becomes the soft cloud that breaks our fall. Such inner strength is also needed to reveal the tender underbelly of ourselves as we aid another person, when being vulnerable brings us in touch with connection. Courage transforms us this way and helps us tune in to the greater consciousness of the All-That-Is, taking us to the edge to find greatness in spite of our fears.

Exercise

In your journal, write the answers to the following questions, giving yourself plenty of time to ponder each in detail. Leave a few blank pages after every one, since you may want to add more thoughts as you move on in the process. It's likely that you'll have new ideas to include as your commitment to the practice of intuition recovery strengthens.

1. During what times in your life have you been courageous?

2. When have you been afraid but taken action anyway?

3. In what capacity do you think courage will be important to your life today?

4. Have you engaged in self-sabotage at any time in your life?

5. Write a list of the times you've acted (or not acted) out of fear, and the consequences for your life.

6. Rewrite the same list with different outcomes, this time choosing to act out of courage. Describe how you'd feel about the new results.

7. How does seeking approval or being a people pleaser sabotage courage?

8. Describe how you may have stayed in an unhealthy situation too long because you couldn't find the courage to change it.

9. Explain how you used courage as a means of changing an unhealthy situation.

10. Is there any part of your life that you feel courage could help you change? Can you make a commitment to change the things you can? What would that entail?

11. When you've had an intuitive hit—a vision of something to come, or an inner knowing that something is going to happen that you could prevent if you changed course—did you act on it or were you afraid to? Do you know why you've been afraid to act on it? Explore these reasons.

12. Do you try to shut down your sixth sense when it's obvious that it's there? Why?

13. What will the people in your life think of you if you tell them that you're opening up to receive more input from your intuition? Does it matter what they think? If so, why?

14. What does *conformity* mean to you?

15. How does your upbringing and your experience (social, religious, cultural, or familial) influence your ability to claim your sixth sense as fully part of your innate humanity?

16. Is courage easy for you to access within yourself? If you feel that some things need to change but are afraid of the consequences, can you ask for help? Imagine requesting that your guardian angel or God give you courage.

17. Explore the following prayer and contemplate how it applies to helping you fully engage in recovering your intuition. How does this prayer apply to freeing oneself from the constant bondage to the ego—the *Me* bubble?

> *God grant me the serenity*
> *to accept the things I cannot change;*
> *courage to change the things I can;*
> *and wisdom to know the difference.*

≫≪ ≫≪ ≫≪

Chapter 19

THE 5TH KEY: FORGIVENESS

For many of us, the greatest blocks to recovering our intuition are found in unresolved resentments and an inability to forgive the past. These not only prevent us from accessing the realm of connection, but also rob us of being in our true present. We aren't able to hear our inner voice clearly when we remain fixed and frozen in the identity of "victim." We can, however, let go and find freedom to be more.

If we're willing to release the underlying self-centered fears that keep us angry, shameful, and filled with contempt for others and ourselves, we can open our hearts, dropping our barriers and invisible walls. Forgiveness becomes a powerful and essential key to finding wholeness, as we begin to realize that our inner conflicts are rooted in our ego-minds and serve to keep us stuck inside our *Me* bubble.

Once we begin the journey of freeing ourselves from the burden of past pain and take responsibility for our part in creating it, our intuition tunes in to the cosmos with uncanny clarity. Each time we decide to forgive someone who's hurt us, we remove a stone from the wall that keeps us separated from our hearts and spirits, as well as their messages. I've witnessed this in my own life, and I see it with my clients each day—a cycle of repeated suffering that can only be healed through forgiveness.

Yet even when we think that we're finished, we might find another, forgotten layer keeping us a prisoner of unmet expectations. There are myriad ways that our Goblins confine us inside our bubbles to relive past hurts over and over. Contemplating and acting on the Key of Forgiveness can be a lifelong, ongoing process for some of us. We may have to learn this the hard way, but it transforms us without question.

Forgiveness is the key to the clarity of our sixth sense because it opens our hearts. Intuition is about tuning in to limitless connection, and forgiveness is like a bridge that's built to take us up out of the *Me* bubble in order to behold the community of the spirit that stretches far into the realm of the All-That-Is. It makes the Goblin inside of us go to sleep and turns up the dial on radio SOUL-FM.

Surrendering the Cycle of Wounding

We know what needs to be forgiven—we see the essence of what must be released repetitively manifesting in our lives. We're trapped in a prison of false perception when we act on thoughts of our wounded past. It's not real . . . it's like we're watching a bad movie that we forgot to take out of the DVD player. While we allow the theme of victim to pervade our identities, we remain in a forgotten and dangerous cave, haunted by the echoes. We can only be fully led out into the light of freedom if we're willing to surrender the swords of self-righteous indignation and the daggers of perpetual wounding.

We must be able to let go of the notion that something horrible happened, which then became a part of us. Instead, we need to learn that we can soar above the pain to see the whole picture and the truth that everything has a purpose for the rich lessons on Earth. We can hear our intuition speak clearly when we accept life exactly as it is and see it as perfect in its imperfection. It's the action of releasing the hurt and all its dark nourishment that allows the light to shine. Our intuition can then tune in to the All-That-Is, showing us what we need to know.

When forgiveness is forgotten, the same hurts find new ways of showing up in our lives over and over, weaving their threads into the fabric of our stories. We then pass these wounds on to people we encounter, just as poison mixes with water, tainting it. We affect others by the state of our minds, which serves to keep us separate and isolated from one another. There will always be consequences for remaining cut off within the bubble, blinded by our conflict. We'll continually see outside of ourselves what we are on the inside. It's up to us to change the DVD and slide in a new and fresh movie, with a different story line that allows us to push the limits of our *Me* bubbles to include much more. I did it—I forgave and so can you!

Exercise

1. In your journal, list all the people whom you feel have harmed you.

2. Rank them according to your perception of their importance. For example, you may want to list your father, your third-grade teacher, or perhaps even yourself. Who do you feel harmed you the

most psychologically, physically, emotionally, or financially?

3. Imagine what it would be like to forgive each one of these individuals, and note any resistance you may have. What will it take for you to practice forgiveness? Make a list. (For example, "It will require *courage* to face my father and forgive him, because he beat me when I was a child"; or "Joe stole money from my brother—I hate him, but I need to free myself from this negative emotion, so it will take a *willingness* to forgive before I can actually do so.")

4. Write a list of how you think forgiveness can make you stronger, more ethical in your own behavior, or more understanding and tolerant of others.

5. How do you feel when you engage in forgiveness? What happens to your perception of the world and your place in it?

6. Whom or what can you never forgive? Why? Contemplate your answer, and pray for the willingness and strength to forgive.

7. Ask yourself what "love" would do.

8. Write down five examples of instances when you were forgiven by someone else. Explain how that changed things between you. How did it make you feel? What was the result of forgiveness? What did you learn?

9. In what way do you feel accountable for your life? Make a list of ten examples.

10. If there were any times in your life when you felt victimized, can you see your part in it? (Be objective: This exercise isn't about blame—it's about getting a clearer perspective on the role that you play in all aspects of your life.)

11. Write a list of events that you can remember when you abdicated responsibility.

12. Jot down a list of your character flaws (such as "I am controlling with my partner," "I tell white lies to suit my interests," or "I take more than my share at dinner").

13. In what ways have you been the cause of suffering for others? Write a list of people you've harmed, you resent, you're angry with, you've lied to, and so on. How do you feel looking at this list? What can you do about it?

14. Note all the people to whom you feel you should make amends. Make those direct apologies, only taking your own part to task, with no opinion about what they've done. (For example, if you owe money and can't settle the whole debt, find your creditor, agree to pay a small amount, and commit to actually doing so; tell the bank teller you snapped at that you're sorry, even if she was rude first; or if you catch yourself in a lie, immediately tell the truth, no matter how ridiculous

you may seem.) Be careful with this step, because sometimes clearing your conscience can harm another.

15. Describe how it feels to practice forgiveness toward others and yourself.

16. Explain how being personally accountable and making amends to those you've harmed relates to the Key of Forgiveness. How does it feel to have practiced it?

≫≪ ≫≪ ≫≪

Chapter 20

THE 6TH KEY: STILLNESS

Stillness is the place where intuition is heard. To find this location in one's consciousness is to encounter the soul, which is always waiting to share its messages and wisdom. Stillness doesn't rely on external silence for it to be accessed. Although quiet places away from our overactive lives are initially crucial to finding it, once we have serenity we must learn to bring it with us. In this way, we're able to keep our intuitive channels clear as we follow our life's path, always tuned in to the cosmos as our constant companion.

Stillness is dependent on maintaining a state of inner mindfulness and a position of detached observation. Finding the peace necessary to hear intuition is like casting a net over the din of life. Then in that place where there's no noise, we can connect to the All-That-Is, which shows us the things we need to know. This location isn't outside of our consciousness, but rather beyond the ego-awareness that keeps us centered on ourselves within the *Me* bubble.

It requires us to let go of the bondage of self and its machi-nations and be contemplative of the greater cosmos—the Divine intelligence—and higher consciousness of the *I Am* presence.

The more we visit that place within us, the more we remember how to get there when our surroundings are chaotic and our minds are clouded. Stillness requires that we commit to practice accessing it, yet it requires us to release our distractions; therefore, doing so is no easy task. We live in a world that feeds on interference and isn't built for stillness. We must learn how to find it in spite of the chaos and fast-tracking high-speed pace of modern life. We need to remember slow, quiet moments—even if it's just the count of one breath—in order to remind us of our soul's existence and the Divine spark of life within and around us. It's important that we take time from our day to be still before we lose ourselves to the busyness of our daily lives.

There are many ways to find stillness. Meditation and prayer are essential steps to doing so, and of course if you're fortunate enough to find a suitable environment in which to practice them, it enhances the experience to go there. I find stillness near water, as it helps me relax, but you may encounter it in a favorite chair, walking in the desert, or sit-ting in a church pew. It can also be found in deep breathing, which allows the surrounding energy of life to fade away with the focus of mindfulness. We can always locate stillness simply by deciding to do so, no matter where we are.

The ability to distinguish the Goblin's chatter from the voice of the authentic, higher consciousness comes with practice. Prayer and meditation in my experience bring in a clear and conscious connection to the Divine, and—as a result—also to the intuitive voice. Even if you're aware that the moment will pass and life will start to impose upon this refuge, you can consciously acknowledge the Divine, your Higher Power, the Universal Intelligence, or God. Stillness keeps us tuned in to limitless connection and is therefore another important key to recovering our intuition.

Finding Peace Within

When we begin our day in stillness, contemplating God in our life, the day goes by in a more manageable fashion. Even if our Goblin self has its tantrums, we have a better chance of calming it down and addressing the issues that have crept up so that a new perspective can emerge in a healthy, inspired, and creative way. In stillness, we know that the Goblin can't hide from us but we can lull it to sleep with hope and the presence of the Divine.

Imagine walking by a calm lake. It feels like moving through a blanket of soft air in a slow-motion movie, and even the way the water gleams is subdued and quiet—it's as if the sun has decided to slow its caress on the surface to be more gentle and loving. For a moment, be aware of the silence and stillness around you. Contemplating it, can you imagine yourself feeling acceptance and allowing whatever needs to be *to be?* Imagine that your mind stops its chatter . . . are you able to feel the peace?

It's not always this calm. Imagine walking by the same lake on a breezy day—when the water is alive and turbulent and the waves dance frenziedly onto the shore, abandoning the stillness for some other music that the gusts bring to life. It reminds you that there's a wildness in our natures that still seeks to connect with the more chaotic creative principle that makes things happen. Nonetheless, you must find a peaceful center to remain grounded in God, the

Divine, and the All-That-Is. Here, you're reminded that stillness isn't located in the outside world. Rather, it needs to be found inside you by allowing the noise and chatter to fall away, leaving you to face your vulnerabilities and gain strength as a result.

We're tested not in the quiet, soft environments of safety, isolated monasteries, or desert retreats. Our trials are in the hustle and bustle of daily life that challenges us to find that still, small voice in spite of the noise. Like the lake, life may be turbulent one moment and quiet the next—whether devastating, restorative, sad, or joyful, nothing remains constant. This makes it that much more important to find an inner stillness and not look to the outside for reassurance.

Meditation—Finding the Type That Works for You

There are many paths to stillness, and meditation is the one I've found to be most effective. I didn't take to it like a duck to water, however: My initial experiences were confusing, awkward, and really uncomfortable at best. In fact, the first time someone introduced me to formal meditation as a concept of spiritual integration through stillness, I was unimpressed. I'm a person who's been in hyper-overdrive since birth, and any attempt to quiet my mind and body was difficult.

I met a man who was an avid devotee of transcendental meditation, and he invited me to come to a class with him. In my first meditation, I found my head to be so busy that I had an anxiety attack. Immediately deciding that this wasn't for me, I went on my quest to find the "right" meditation. I visited a Tibetan temple, a Zen Buddhist group, a self-proclaimed avatar who was giving classes in meditation, and the Unity Church. I found the same thing each time: My mind was crowded, loud, and preoccupied with my Goblin—and a few of its relatives that I didn't even know I had. But I needed to start somewhere, and guided meditation was the place I began.

The first time I was led through such a meditation was with a recording by Shakti Gawain from her book *Creative Visualization.* I found focusing on her voice soothing and calming; and the exercise was very effective, grounding, and relaxing. I noticed immediately that the stillness was clarifying and had dimmed my inner chaos. It somehow made it easier to access my intuition, although I hadn't expected that result. When I added this guided-relaxation technique to accompany my prayers, I was better able to function, both in my day-to-day life and when I used my intuitive gift for others.

If you have trouble meditating, find a guided-meditation CD to listen to each day. This can be highly effective, especially in the beginning. I also find that listening to music that's accompanied by the sound of waves helps immensely. My favorites have the ocean as a background to ambient music—this is the way that I recorded *Journey Through the Chakras* and *I Am/Grace.* I believe that this speaks to our beginnings, since we're all made from water and moved and pulled by the moon. Perhaps memories of Atlantis whisper to our psyches, asking us to drop our defenses and expand our consciousness to include the vastness of spirit. Regardless of my imaginative mystical theories, I know that this meditation technique works.

An alternative (and just as effective) way to find stillness is in the slow counting of breath. The word *spirit* comes from the Latin *spirare,* which means "to breathe." When we count each inhalation and exhalation, we acknowledge that we're spirit first and human second—this allows us to feel the freedom that stillness brings. Slowing down and finding a moment of peace in our day brings us closer to our authentic selves and allows us a moment to catch our breath. In the stillness, we can *know* where we are and where we should go next.

With practice, stillness can be experienced clearly without undue effort. We can learn how to hear and feel, as well as where to look for, the answers that it brings. When we find them, we know that we're home inside our own skin, no matter what challenges the world presents. Stillness allows us to connect to our intuition. Regardless of what the day brings, we can remain centered in the commitment to surrender and allow things to unfold as they should—in stillness, we can know peace. And as we recall the Divine Source of all life, we're also able to remember the future.

Exercise

1. Do you take time out from your day to be still and quiet? In your journal, list all the reasons why you do or don't.

2. Imagine a beautiful, still, quiet place. What does it look like? What are the elements that you identify with the principle of stillness?

3. Practice emptying your mind of all thoughts. Let them go, as if they were leaves drifting on a river. Slow your breathing down, and take a series of deep breaths. List all the benefits you receive from the experience.

4. Make a commitment to meditate for a minimum of 15 minutes each day. For one month, keep track of when you practice it and when you don't. (This isn't a test, only a method to track results.) Notice the difference on the days when you meditate versus the ones when you don't. Write them down.

5. Practice asking for God's guidance when you're still—after all, stillness is about listening. What do you hear in your mind when you're quiet? If you receive any messages, write them down. Always ask for the guidance that would be for the highest good of all concerned. (For example, your intuition would never tell you to go rob a bank if you're broke; instead, it would say, *Call Jim,* who would tell you about a job prospect.)

6. Be willing to learn about the subject of meditation. Go to a bookstore and browse some of the titles devoted to this subject. See which one appeals to you, and make a commitment to read it all the way through.

7. List why you believe that meditation is important to recovering intuition. What are the benefits of accessing your sixth sense? What "rewards" do you receive by not doing so? (For example: "If I remain closed to my intuition, I'll fit in and appear normal.")

⇒≪ ⇒≪ ⇒≪

Chapter 21

THE 7TH KEY: LOVE

Love paves the way on the road to recovering intuition, as it tunes us in to the limitless connection that dissolves the barriers of separation and is something to truly appreciate and respect. As we contemplate this key, we think it, feel it, and then learn to live it. Our minds serve to analyze our experience, but our hearts immerse us in love . . . it's the experience of a compassionate heart.

Love is freedom from fear and all the other things that keep us prisoners in our solitary bubbles. It's unconditional, accepting, inclusive, joining, uniting, and sharing. Love is an act of kindness, and compassion is its companion. It puts to rest the Goblin inside us and brings a sense of safety and peace to its slumber. Once the Goblin is understood, it can only be released through caring, as understanding alone isn't enough. Love is the solution that releases the constraints of the ego-mind, along with its tight hold on the separated identity that interferes with intuition.

Love is more than just an expression between people— on its own, it's a dimension of awareness. As a key to recovering intuition, this has a greater meaning than the love between two individuals, which is romantic, subjective, often possessive, and subject to intrinsic conditions. Love as a key is about a consciousness of infinite connection and potential, along with being open to achieving the highest and best possibilities for yourself and others. It's about respecting every other creature and object, recognizing and supporting their greatest potential as well.

This is no easy task: We live in a divisive and inequitable global culture where war is always imminent and poverty is an ever-growing blight on the world. Racial prejudice, religious differences, and economic and ecological imbalances give many of us illusory reasons to remain in our bubbles. So what would happen if we *really* loved—that is, with no conditions, inclusive of all? What would become of the differences that have enabled some of us to broker power and influence? What occurs then? Is it worth it? What's the cost and what's the benefit?

Love pops our bubbles and makes us personally vulnerable, but it also connects us to the suffering of the collective human condition and the responsibility it implies. The price is high, but the payoff is great, as we embrace the deep sense of connection that can only be experienced once the bubbles that separate us have been burst open. With love, we wake up to the truth of the All-That-Is, the Divine creative principle that only knows a unified sense of being. This is the truth of all things: Our highest, most spiritual existence is made of the essence of love. When we contemplate this, we're reminded of the equal right of every sentient being on the planet to transcend suffering and achieve happiness. Love is always the answer, because it's the only reality . . . the rest is illusion.

Love—a Celebration of Diversity

Intuition is the innate reminder that in recovering our connection to a greater awareness, we also regain a sense that everyone else is the *same* as us, instead of calculating our *differences*. We learn to identify with others, rather than comparing ourselves to them and competing with them. Love, the awareness of the heart, allows for and celebrates diversity. It's not easy, but it can be done—every teeny bit makes a difference. When love is our focus, life is smoother, and we see miracles as we're released from fear, which is always a construct of the thinking mind, not of the spirit. When we engage our sixth sense, we pull in information with clean curiosity, devoid of prejudice, and therefore we can interpret with clarity. Our filters gather much less debris when love is the key that we contemplate and act upon.

Intuition is *seen, felt, heard,* and *known* because of love. There's an undeniable connection between the sixth sense and the heart. The more we open it and our spirits, the greater our clarity as we finely tune our awareness to SOUL-FM. The path to recovering intuition is about tuning in to this universal unlimited connection. And when we regain this ability, we're consciously and purposefully tuning in to God.

Exercise

1. In your journal, write out a definition of *love,* outlining its attributes.

2. List the characteristics of romantic love.

3. Describe the love that parents have for their children, and vice versa.

4. Explain the affection between a person and his or her pet.

5. What are the differences between all of the above forms of love?

6. *Why* are there differences?

7. If God is love, what does that mean to you?

8. In contemplating limitless connection, how is love a factor in All-That-Is? How does it relate to the manner in which we treat each other?

9. When we tune in to love, what happens to fear?

10. When was the last time you performed a random act of kindness? Explain how it felt.

11. Commit to doing an anonymous act of kindness each day. For example, take your neighbor's garbage to the curb without telling her it was you, or buy a coffee for the next person in line at the coffee shop or drive-through. Write down how you felt after doing this.

12. Explore your racial prejudices: Why do you have them? Can you view other people as being the same as you are? How do you feel when you do so?

13. Sit down comfortably in a chair or your favorite
    meditation spot, and close your eyes. Inhale and
    exhale deeply and slowly for 15 breaths. Bring
    your attention to your heart center, and imagine
    that each time you take a breath, you're inhal-
    ing all the love in the universe. Let it fill you
    completely until every cell in your body is buzz-
    ing with this energy. Now imagine that you have
    a special transmitter inside your heart that can
    beam love out to others. Visualize sending this
    powerful energy to every sentient being in the
    universe, as well as each rock, leaf, and inani-
    mate object, since all of nature is actually alive
    with energy. Experience how you feel and write it
    down.

14. Here's a daily spot check: Throughout the day,
    peek into your heart center. Are you feeling open,
    loving, inclusive, and expansive? If instead you're
    tight and constrained, what's causing this? You
    might need to release your Goblin, so take a mini-
    break and spend a bit of time lulling it to sleep.
    Explain how it feels to show yourself love and
    compassion in this way.

➤◄ ➤◄ ➤◄

Chapter 22

INTUITION PRACTICE EXERCISES

The practices included in this chapter represent the basic tools that you'll need to help you on the path to recover your intuition. I've designed them to aid you in the process of discovering your own innate six-sensory gift and have used them as basic foundational exercises during my popular seminars on developing intuition. I also practice them myself on a regular basis. After completing them, you'll be amazed by all that you are, as well as everything that you're able to perceive outside of your five senses. Remember to keep an open mind and be willing to learn, suspend judgment, and be patient.

The best way to do the exercises is in order, starting with creating your sacred environment, followed by finding your Sanctuary. Once you've consistently found that you're able to create your inner Sanctuary, move on to the next part. The Net exercise can be done anytime, anywhere, and as many times as you need to. Practice makes perfect, and as the Nike commercials say: "Just do it."

175

Your Sacred Environment

Before you begin, it's important to create a sacred space in which to do these meditation exercises to aid you on your path to recover your intuition. Make sure that the space is private and secure and you feel safe there—it's critical that you remain undisturbed for at least 30 minutes. Returning to the same place again and again will assist you in establishing an inner environment that's safe and grounded, one you can return to every day for meditation, whether or not you're physically in your sacred space. This will help you stay present so that you don't "space out."

You can also use meditation music—in fact, I recommend that you do. It's best to listen to the same music each time you practice the exercise that you choose to accompany it. Your mind will recognize it as a key to the inner door that you wish to open, allowing a quicker access to your intuitive voice as it relays its messages to you. The best music to use includes the rhythmic sound of waves, either from a lake or the ocean. Of course, in my other career as a recording artist, I've created a number of CDs along these lines, as have many other artists. Whichever you decide on, just remember that the music must be soothing and mellow—if there are drums, the best beat is repetitive, with very little variance.

Candles may be lit and incense burned, if you choose. Try to do these exercises in the same physical place every day, such as in a particular chair or room. Consistency and familiarity are helpful because you become used to the environment and won't have to acclimate each time you begin.

Finding Your Sanctuary

The purpose of this section is to find an image of a sacred space that you can visit every time you do one of these exercises. I've found such a visualization important to this process, as the Sanctuary becomes the doorway to your experience of receiving information through your intuitive gifts and is crucial to tuning in to your inner radio.

Sit comfortably in your sacred environment, breathing deeply and relaxing your body. Allow your mind to let go of the events of the day, imagining each scene or thought floating away in a bubble of white light. Now imagine that you're walking on a path of smooth crystal stone. A tiny globe of white light floats in front of you and asks you to follow it. Allow your imagination to see the path lead you into natural surroundings, such as a white sandy beach beside an enchanted ocean or a waterfall in a secluded glen by an ancient forest.

Breathe deeply, and imagine that your entire being is filled with sparkling white light. Each time you inhale, the light comes in, and as you exhale, a great cloud of darkness and negative energy goes out. As you're breathing, allow your imagination to explore the special place inside your mind that will be your Sanctuary. Let your awareness send out an intention so that this vision of inner peace will become sacred to you and only accessible by you, your guardian angel, or any other spiritual guides of the highest nature. Here you'll be safe, secure, and receptive to your soul, feeling relaxed, calm, and at one with all things. This is your personal Sanctuary.

With your eyes closed, spend some time in your Sanctuary getting to know this sacred space. Remember to breathe deeply and slowly as your body relaxes and your mind finds peace here. After about 15 minutes, open your eyes and experience how you feel, having found your Sanctuary.

It's handy to keep a journal each time you enter this place, making note of any changes that may occur in the Sanctuary. Once a week, see if you can notice any consistent patterns that may symbolically relate to the issues of your daily life.

It's preferable that you visit your Sanctuary daily in meditation for a minimum of 15 to 30 minutes over the course of one week to get accustomed to it. It's the location of your inner awareness, where you'll explore your intuition and the messages that you tune in to from the All-That-Is.

Grounding Exercise

Sit in a comfortable chair, with your feet firmly planted on the ground. Close your eyes and imagine that you're breathing in a circular motion. With each breath, fill yourself with light, and release all the tension in your body as you exhale. Keep doing this until the rhythm of your breathing slows down after about five minutes. Sense the weight of your body becoming heavier in the chair.

Now imagine that you're like a tree growing roots that reach deep into the center of the earth and extend from the base of your spine and the soles of your feet. In your mind's eye, see the roots drawing up vital life-force energy from the earth, and visualize it circulating through your body and every cell, up and around, then returning back down. Experience the sensation of being rooted, grounded, and a part of the natural energy that connects us all. Send your love and gratitude to the earth and the Divine intelligence inherent in all life, noticing how you feel.

Opening the Channels

The most powerful exercise I've found to open the natural receptors to intuitive information is a meditation that focuses on opening and clearing the seven energy centers of the mind/body/spirit called the "chakras." As I've explained, this is a philosophical system that comes to us from Eastern culture. Originally presented through the practice of yoga—a holistic physical and mental discipline that serves to "yoke together" the Divine and the individual—the chakra system for healing and well-being has now become popular in the West.

The chakras represent seven steps of ever-expanding states of consciousness and serve to describe spinning wheels of energy that are stacked one on top of the other in a column that spans from the base of the spine to the top of the head. The wheels that are said to exist within us correspond to the seven colors of the rainbow and the seven musical notes of the Western C scale. (My CD *Journey Through the Chakras* was created specifically based on this system for the purpose of guiding the listener through an intuitive-development exercise.)

Rather than go into too much detail, I'll suggest a couple of books if you want to study the chakras further. *Anatomy of the Spirit,* by Caroline Myss; and *Eastern Body, Western Mind,* by Anodea Judith were the two books I studied that most influence my work and my own personal experiences with meditation and the chakras. However, you don't need an intellectual reference point to experience the benefits of this visualization exercise. Even before I knew the meaning of the wheels of light, I was activating them in my inner awareness, and this had a profound effect on me. I felt clear, energized, and balanced; and I was able to experience a consistent heightened awareness of my intuitive gifts as a result of engaging in the meditation.

Here's one of my favorite visualization exercises to open the channels of awareness. Sit comfortably in a chair, feet apart and on the ground, and breathe deeply and slowly for a count of 30. Find your Sanctuary and get acquainted with your sacred environment. Imagine a rainbow of light forming directly in front of you. Observe the pure, bright colors of red, orange, yellow, green, blue, violet, and white. Now invite each color in succession to envelop you with sparkling, brilliant light, one by one:

1. **Red:** Let the color swirl around you. Invite it to be absorbed into your being until it's drawn into a spinning wheel of red light at the base of your spine.

2. **Orange:** Let the color swirl around you. Then draw the light into a spinning wheel of orange just below your belly button.

3. **Yellow:** Let the color swirl around you. Then draw the yellow light into a spinning wheel of pulsing illumination at your solar plexus, just below your rib cage.

4. **Green:** Let the color swirl around you. Envelop yourself with beautiful, clear green light, drawing it into a spinning wheel of emerald in the center of your chest.

5. **Blue:** Let the color swirl around you. Surround yourself with sparkling blue light, drawing it into

a spinning wheel of sapphire energy in the center of your throat.

6. **Violet:** Let the color swirl around you. Invite the light to be absorbed into your being as a spinning wheel of bright purple light in the center of your forehead.

7. **White:** Let the color swirl around you. Imagine that you're surrounded by pure white light. Invite the light to be absorbed through your body, and then draw it into a spinning wheel of brilliant white energy at the top of your head.

Give thanks to the rainbow and open your eyes. Keep a journal of your experience with each color every time you do this exercise. How do you feel? Do you receive any messages? Images? Feelings? Sounds?

Ideally, for the first couple weeks you'll do this meditation daily, keeping tabs on your experience with each color as you go. I prefer that you *not* study the meanings in advance, because I want you to experience the exercise first, learning how to decipher the experience intuitively. You can add the intellectual content later.

After I'd done emotional, psychological, and spiritual cleanup and started these practical exercises, I began to see my gift expand in a manner that spoke to me in my own inner language, which I later investigated logically. Remember that intuition doesn't follow the same rules that our other senses do and cannot be intellectualized and studied in the same way as other subjects. So I'm suggesting an almost backward way of learning here: Experience it first and learn about it later. The most difficult time you'll have is when you think that you grasp what you're doing. I'm asking you to forget what you believe you know and surrender to another way of experiencing the world. If you always remember to ask God to keep you in the light, you'll never become lost in the dark.

The Net

This is my favorite exercise to "collect" information from my intuition. I practice it when I prepare for a reading, as well as when I'm out in the world and need to seek unseen clues about the happenings that may surround me or those I love.

Relax comfortably, eyes closed, and prepare yourself with the grounding exercise that you learned early on. Afterward, bring your awareness into a rolled-up net of energy that appears in your hands. Imagine that you're in the center of an ocean of sparkling water that's filled with the memories of everything—every thought, every word spoken, and every action taken or contemplated. All possible causes and effects ever in existence—past, present, or future—are there like magical fish swimming among buried treasure.

Imagine casting your energy net into this sea of awareness. Pull the net in and see what you've caught in it. Don't judge it if you don't immediately recognize what you've found. It can sometimes take awhile to decipher your personal intuitive language. Messages may come to you as a "flash" of knowledge, factual information such as a number, a visual image, an emotional experience, a feeling in your solar plexus, a physical sensation, or an inner voice or sound.

Keep a journal of what you encounter, and observe how the meanings and messages found in your energy net correspond to your outer world.

Exploring Your Personal
Relationship to the Mystery of Spirit

1. Using your journal, explore your relationship to a Higher Power (or God). How do you see this relationship unfold in your daily life?

2. How do you view God? Is the Divine everywhere? Is there a Higher Power in nature? Is God within you or only outside of you? Write down a list of attributes that you view God as possessing.

3. Where did you first learn about God? Write down your earliest memories of how the Creator was introduced to you.

4. Explore how your relationship with the Divine has changed. If it hasn't, write down why that's so.

5. Do you pray? How? What do you expect from prayer?

6. Do you believe in angels or spirit guides? Write down why or why not.

7. Explore your relationship to your intuition. Do you trust it? Record five examples when you had

faith that was accurate, as well as five instances when you didn't, explaining what happened.

8. Do you have faith in yourself? What does that mean to you?

9. Describe faith as an action. What does that action entail?

10. Write a list of things or people you have faith in and why.

11. If you struggle with a dogmatic religious relationship to a Higher Power, how can you engage in a spiritual life that accepts that there are many paths to the Divine? Can you keep your heart and mind open to allow others to believe as they do and still keep the integrity of your faith?

12. Can you accept that the sixth sense is a natural part of your humanity?

13. What does the ability to access nonlocal reality mean to you?

14. What does unlimited connection have to do with personal responsibility and morality?

15. What does "keeping an open mind" mean to you?

16. What commitment are you willing to make to help create a better world?

Afterword

I stood on the beach today and saw something truly amazing. It was very windy, sand was blowing in all directions, and it was hard to walk. In spite of that, a lone monarch butterfly with delicate orange and black wings flew in front of me and miraculously suspended herself, as if the wind weren't even blowing. I marveled at the fact that the breeze was no match for her. How strong she must have been to hold her own so effortlessly in the midst of such seemingly fierce elements.

Autumn marks the beginning of the monarch butterfly's migration south. To escape the cold snowy season ahead, these creatures will leave Canada and journey down to Mexico, where they'll be safe and protected throughout the winter months. Did you know that it actually could take the span of up to three generations of monarchs to make the entire trek back to Toronto from Mexico? On the way up after the winter, one generation dies after giving birth to another that intuitively knows how to continue the journey northward. That generation may also perish along the way and be followed by a third, which finally makes it to the ultimate destination. Although each generation only sees a small portion of the journey, they all collectively contribute—and more remarkably, they all *know how* to do so—to the larger plan for their survival.

Maybe that's what our collective *human* journey is about. Our quest is one that's intuitively known because of those that came before. Perhaps that's what all of life is about, showing that even as our mortal bodies perish, there's strength in our inherent nature as spiritual beings to continue life, passing on what we've learned from one generation to the next in order to help each of us find our way home. The thing that connects us, the attribute that leads us home, is inside of us—it's our intuition. I've always believed that it was given to us as a kind of homing device to remind us that as spirit, we always belong.

This book is dedicated to every person who's reached out beyond the bubble in search of meaning.

⪼⪻ ⪼⪻ ⪼⪻

Acknowledgments

The birth of this book had many special angels, elves, and fairies in "people suits," coaxing it to life, and I would like to thank you all from the bottom of my heart.

A very special thanks to Denise Linn for your extraordinary support and enthusiastic friendship over all these years. Thank you for holding my hand through the most difficult stage of my book! You have been my shining light, and I send you oodles of love and gratitude.

For the early days, a very special thank you to Yvonne Oswald for pointing the way.

To Tessa Graham—your enthusiastic efforts and belief in me and my message gave this book its wings. Lucky us—to be gifted with an undying friendship as a bonus. Blessed be! And thank you to Kevin West for writing such a great article about me in *W* that got Tessa's attention!

Thank you to Louise Hay for being the pioneer who brought new thought to the world and changed the face of publishing by creating Hay House. You provide those of us who would normally be considered too far outside the mainstream a safe, secure, and credible platform from which to share our ideas with grace and respectability. I will be eternally grateful to you. Thank you for also being the coolest, hippest woman with the best laugh.

And thanks to Ron Tillinghast—a big, giant kiss of gratitude. You rock.

Thank you to Reid Tracy, president and CEO of Hay House, whom I continue to ask, "You sure you don't have wings tucked in your jacket?" Thank you for the phenomenal opportunity to share my message and for always giving me the best advice. Thank you for your patience, wisdom, and sense of humor, and for letting me think it's all been my idea.

Special thanks to Stacey Smith, my little miracle; my pal Jill Kramer; Shannon Littrell; Amy Rose Grigoriou; Adrian Sandoval; Roberta Grace; and the rest of the Hay House family—too numerous to name. You are all so important, and I send you oodles of gratitude.

Thank you to Summer McStravick and the crew at **HayHouseRadio.com**. Thanks also to Sonny, Joe, Kyle, and Diane—you make my Thursdays so meaningful! And a big hug to WS radio for guiding my baby steps to radio.

To my master editorial angels, Janice Zawerbny and Laura Nenych—thanks for your guidance, understanding, patience, and genius (and for keeping me from eating too many cookies).

Thank you to my awesome assistant, Michelle Morgan. I don't know how I functioned without you! Thanks to Carla Eide and my wonderful former assistant, Vicki DeLiberato, with so much appreciation.

Thanks to my magical Fairy Cheering Section for your support and great opinions along the way as you tolerated my sharing the book with you in progress—Michael Alaska, Alex Bennett, Gillian and David Lowe, Courtney Taylor, Jeffrey Kong, Natalie Osborne, Victoria Valius, Nancy Scott-Ainsley, Sophie Craighead, Victoria Pearman, Kim White, Karen Gordon, Steven Ehrlick, Julie Brown, Cheryl Richardson, and my great friend Justine Picardie.

Thank you to my dearest friend, business partner, and Cosmic Cookie sister, soul-pal Deenah Dunkleman-Mollin. You are my shining light!

Thanks to Debra Samuel for your friendship, the way you help me see beauty in the world, and for making me look so good in photos (and slimmer, too!). Thanks also to Beth Richards—you have a place in my heart always.

Thank you to Sylvia Browne and John Holland, with so much love for your generosity and warm welcome to the psychic experience at sea!

Thanks to my long-lost soul-sister Nancy Levin. How fabulous are you!

Thanks to everyone at Worldview Travel.

Thank you to the women at the Saturday-morning meeting and Monday night at the Hill for keeping me sane and grounded.

A special thanks to Marguerite Lee, Marg Muir, and Heather Truster—my special guides and spiritual mentors—and to Dr. Karen Klopecki for inspiring me with your wisdom and grace.

Thank you to the following angelic beings (in no particular order): my wonderful supportive friends Lance and Tricia Secretan—a very special thanks, Gerry Mosbyn, Chrissie Young, Kimme Myles, Maureen Ford, Gari-Ellen Brick, Heather Dietrich, Elley-Ray Hennessey, Rebecca Richards and Angie, Kate, Carol Thibault, Nanci Harris, Nahanni Johnston, Shante Paige, Suzanne Boyd, Ian

Rebecca Richards and Angie, Kate, Carol Thibault, Nanci Harris, Nahanni Johnston, Shante Paige, Suzanne Boyd, Ian Hilton, Shelley Von Strunckel, Bina Sella, Teresa Hale, Caroline Stanley, Atoosa Salimi, Jeffrey Kong, Loretta Munoz, Althea Grey, Jill Feinberg, Dr. Nitin DiLawri, Steven and Elyse Aronoff, Debra Silverman, Judi Beane, Cecil Kramer, Diana Dickson, Gerry Mosby and Pam Fenton, Gina McWade, Lisa Fein, Bettina Zilka, Kate Ford, Tony Nolasco, Julie Gibson, Elena Saldini, Dana Joon, Shannon Ferguson, Sharon Kirkham, Steve Reid, Anna Sachs, Meadow Linn, and anyone I might have missed—if you think you belong on this list, you absolutely do and I love you.

To Deane Cameron, president of EMI Music Canada, a zillion special thanks for taking a risk and listening to your intuition. Special thanks to Warren Stewart and Tim Trombley, Fraser Hill.

A special thanks to Salim Khoja, Art and David Sersta from Power Within, Ron Szymanski, and everyone at Fresh Partners, London, U.K. And hugs to Dr. Noel Solish and Dr. Linda Yolles.

Thanks to Eric Rosse for inspiring me beyond measure, and to Mars Lasar, Rob DeBoer, and Tony Grace for your music, magic, and mastery. How lucky am I to have such awesome creative partners!

Thank you to the thousands of extraordinary people who have sat for readings with me over these years and allowed me access to their lives—past, present, and future. You have helped shape what I am and what I have come to believe. You have truly given meaning to my life.

Thanks to Olly, my spirit guide; and that 30-foot angel I see once in a while; and whoever else is around, guiding me all these years. Thanks to God, Goddess, and the Mystery, etc. I'm privileged to be part of the human-spirit dance again. I hope that I get it right this time.

Finally, the most special thanks of all to the love of my life, Marc Lindeman; and our babies, Sabbi and Bizoo. You have inspired me; supported me; loved me; and given me safety, freedom, integrity, and the family I have always wanted. I'm the luckiest girl on the planet.

※ ※ ※

Bibliography

These are some of the books that have influenced and informed my ideas and knowledge on the subject of spirituality and intuition.

Anonymous. *Alcoholics Anonymous*. New York: Alcoholics Anonymous World Services, Inc., 1976.

Borysenko, Joan. *A Woman's Journey to God*. New York: Riverhead Books, 1999.

Gawain, Shakti. *Creative Visualization*. Berkeley, California: Whatever Publishing, 1978.

Huxley, Aldous. *The Perennial Philosophy: An Interpretation of the Great Mystics, East and West*. New York: Harper & Brothers Publishers, 1945.

Jennings, Jesse, ed. *The Essential Ernest Holmes*. New York: Jeremy P. Tarcher/Putnam, 2002.

Judith, Anodea. *Eastern Body, Western Mind: Psychology and the Chakra System as a Path to the Self*. Berkeley, California: Celestial Arts Publishing, 1996.

Loveland-Coen, Victoria. *Manifesting Your Desires*. Sherman Oaks, California: Self-Mastery Press, 1995.

Moore, Thomas. *Care of the Soul.* New York: HarperCollins Publishers, Inc., 1992.

Myss, Caroline. *Anatomy of the Spirit: Seven Stages of Power and Healing.* New York: Three Rivers Press, 1996.

Orloff, Judith, M.D. *Second Sight.* New York: Warner Books, Inc., 1996.

Ouspensky, P. D. *In Search of the Miraculous.* New York: Harcourt, Inc., 1949.

Peck, M. Scott, M.D. *The Road Less Traveled.* New York: Touchstone, 1978.

Ponder, Catherine. *The Dynamic Laws of Prayer.* Marina del Rey, California: DeVorss & Company, 1987.

Price, John Randolph. *Practical Spirituality.* Carlsbad, California: Hay House, Inc., 1996.

Roberts, Jane. *The Nature of Personal Reality: A Seth Book.* San Rafael, California: Amber-Allen Publishing, Inc., 1994.

Roman, Sanaya. *Personal Power Through Awareness.* Tiburon, California: HJ Kramer, Inc., 1986.

Shinn, Florence Scovel. *The Wisdom of Florence Scovel Shinn.* New York: Fireside, 1989.

Stein, Diane. *All Women Are Psychics.* Berkeley, California: The Crossing Press, 1988.

Steiner, Rudolf. *How to Know Higher Worlds.* New York: Anthroposophic Press, Inc., 1994.

Talbot, Michael. *The Holographic Universe.* New York: HarperCollins Publishers, Inc., 1991.

Targ, Russell and Jane Katra, Ph.D. *Miracles of Mind.* Novato, California: New World Library, 1998.

Wilson, Colin. *Mysteries.* London: Granada Publishing, Ltd., 1979.

≫≪ ≫≪ ≫≪

About the Author

Colette Baron-Reid is a popular spiritual intuitive, seminar leader, radio personality, motivational speaker, and musical recording artist on the EMI music label (with a top-selling meditation CD, *Journey Through the Chakras*). She has shared the stage with authors Sylvia Browne, John Holland, Caroline Myss, and many others. She currently lives in Toronto, Canada, with her husband and their two furry children. Website: **www.colettebaronreid.com**

≫≪ ≫≪ ≫≪

"To enhance your experience of this book, I invite you to join the members' lounge at **www.colettebaronreid. com.** For the *Remembering the Future* interactive book site and community, download 13 FREE meditations, FREE video lessons, a FREE daily oracle, a prayer board forum, and more!"

Many blessings from the heart,
Colette

NOTES

NOTES

NOTES

NOTES

NOTES

NOTES

.

We hope you enjoyed this Hay House book. If you'd like to receive a free catalog featuring additional Hay House books and products, or if you'd like information about the Hay Foundation, please contact:

Hay House, Inc.
P.O. Box 5100
Carlsbad, CA 92018-5100

(760) 431-7695 or **(800) 654-5126**
(760) 431-6948 (fax) or **(800) 650-5115 (fax)**
www.hayhouse.com® • **www.hayfoundation.org**

Published and distributed in Australia by: Hay House Australia Pty. Ltd., 18/36 Ralph St., Alexandria NSW 2015 • *Phone:* 612-9669-4299 *Fax:* 612-9669-4144 • www.hayhouse.com.au

Published and distributed in the United Kingdom by: Hay House UK, Ltd., 292B Kensal Rd., London W10 5BE • *Phone:* 44-20-8962-1230 *Fax:* 44-20-8962-1239 • www.hayhouse.co.uk

Published and distributed in the Republic of South Africa by: Hay House SA (Pty), Ltd., P.O. Box 990, Witkoppen 2068 *Phone/Fax:* 27-11-467-8904 • orders@psdprom.co.za • www.hayhouse.co.za

Published in India by: Hay House Publishers India, Muskaan Complex, Plot No. 3, B-2, Vasant Kunj, New Delhi 110 070 *Phone:* 91-11-4176-1620 • *Fax:* 91-11-4176-1630 • www.hayhouse.co.in

Distributed in Canada by: Raincoast, 9050 Shaughnessy St., Vancouver, B.C. V6P 6E5 • *Phone:* (604) 323-7100 *Fax:* (604) 323-2600 • www.raincoast.com

Tune in to **HayHouseRadio.com®** for the best in inspirational talk radio featuring top Hay House authors! And, sign up via the Hay House USA Website to receive the Hay House online newsletter and stay informed about what's going on with your favorite authors. You'll receive bimonthly announcements about: Discounts and Offers, Special Events, Product Highlights, Free Excerpts, Giveaways, and more! **www.hayhouse.com®**